CW01011106

Introducing Teachers' Writing Groups

Teachers' writing groups have a significantly positive impact on pupils and their writing. This timely text explains the importance of teachers' writing groups and how they have evolved. It outlines clearly and accessibly how teachers can set up their own highly effective writing groups.

In this practical and informative book, the authors:

- share the thinking and practice that is embodied by teachers' writing groups;
- provide practical support for teachers running a group or wishing to write for themselves in order to inform their practice;
- cover major themes such as: the relationship between writing teachers and the teaching of writing; writing as process and pleasure; writing and reflective practice; writing journals and the writing workshop.

The authors provide a rationale for the development of writing groups for teachers and for ways of approaching writing that support adult and child writers, and this rationale informs the ideas for writing throughout the book. All writing and teaching suggestions have been extensively tried and tested by class teachers and will be of enormous interest to any teacher or teacher educator wishing to run their own successful writing group.

Jenifer Smith is Senior Lecturer in Education and Lifelong Learning at the University of East Anglia, UK.

Simon Wrigley is a retired English Adviser (Bedfordshire and Buckinghamshire) and former Chair of the National Association for the Teaching of English, UK.

NATE

The National Association for the Teaching of English (NATE), founded in 1963, is the professional body for all teachers of English from primary to Post-16. Through its regions, committees and conferences, the association draws on the work of classroom practitioners, advisers, consultants, teacher trainers, academics and researchers to promote dynamic and progressive approaches to the subject by means of debate, training and publications. NATE is a charity reliant on membership subscriptions. If you teach English in any capacity, please visit **www.nate.org.uk** and consider joining NATE, so the association can continue its work and give teachers of English and the subject a strong voice nationally.

This series of books co-published with NATE reflects the organisation's dedication to promoting standards of excellence in the teaching of English, from early years through to university level. Titles in this series promote innovative and original ideas that have practical classroom outcomes and support teachers' own professional development.

Books in the NATE series include both pupil and classroom resources and academic research aimed at English teachers, students on PGCE/ITT courses and NQTs.

Titles in this series include:

International Perspectives on Teaching English in a Globalised World
Andrew Goodwyn, Louann Reid and Cal Durrant

Teaching English Language 16–19
Martin Illingworth and Nick Hall

Unlocking Poetry (CD-ROM)
Trevor Millum and Chris Warren

Teaching English Literature 16–19
Carol Atherton, Andrew Green and Gary Snapper

Teaching Caribbean Poetry
Beverley Bryan and Morag Styles

Sharing not Staring, 2nd Edition
Trevor Millum and Chris Warren

Teaching Grammar Structure and Meaning
Marcello Giovanelli

Researching and Teaching Reading
Gabrielle Cliff Hodges

Introducing Teachers' Writing Groups
Jenifer Smith and Simon Wrigley

Creative Approaches to Teaching Grammar
Martin Illingworth and Nick Hall

Introducing Teachers' Writing Groups

Exploring the theory and practice

Jenifer Smith and Simon Wrigley

Routledge
Taylor & Francis Group
LONDON AND NEW YORK

NATE

First published 2016
by Routledge
2 Park Square, Milton Park, Abingdon, Oxon OX14 4RN

and by Routledge
711 Third Avenue, New York, NY 10017

Routledge is an imprint of the Taylor & Francis Group, an informa business

© 2016 J. Smith & S. Wrigley

The right of J. Smith & S. Wrigley to be identified as authors of this work has been asserted by them in accordance with sections 77 and 78 of the Copyright, Designs and Patents Act 1988.

All rights reserved. No part of this book may be reprinted or reproduced or utilised in any form or by any electronic, mechanical, or other means, now known or hereafter invented, including photocopying and recording, or in any information storage or retrieval system, without permission in writing from the publishers.

Trademark notice: Product or corporate names may be trademarks or registered trademarks, and are used only for identification and explanation without intent to infringe.

British Library Cataloguing in Publication Data
A catalogue record for this book is available from the British Library

Library of Congress Cataloging-in-Publication Data
Names: Smith, Jenifer, author. | Wrigley, Simon, author.
Title: Introducing teachers' writing groups : exploring the theory and practice / Jenifer Smith and Simon Wrigley.
Description: Abingdon, Oxon ; New York, NY : Routledge, 2016.
Identifiers: LCCN 2015023445 | ISBN 9781138797420 (hardback : alk. paper) | ISBN 9781138797437 (pbk. : alk. paper) | ISBN 9781315757155 (ebook)
Subjects: LCSH: Language arts teachers—In-service training. | Language arts teachers—Professional relationships. | Composition (Language arts)—Study and teaching. | Authorship—Collaboration. | Group work in education.
Classification: LCC LB1743 .S65 2016 | DDC 370.71/1—dc23
LC record available at http://lccn.loc.gov/2015023445

ISBN: 978-1-138-79742-0 (hbk)
ISBN: 978-1-138-79743-7 (pbk)
ISBN: 978-1-315-75715-5 (ebk)

Typeset in Galliard
by Apex CoVantage, LLC

For writing teachers

Contents

Acknowledgements

Although we have written the bulk of this text, we have done so alongside and supported by many voices. We hope that the reader can hear those voices loud and clear. We especially thank the following people whose words, ideas and practice can be found throughout the book:

Lynwen Allen, Helen Atkinson, Andrea Ball, Daniel Barnes, Cat Barr, Martin Batchelor, Jane Bluett, Emma Bodsworth, Janet Bremer, Sam Brewer, Susan Brice, Clare Bristow, Ruth Buckland, Marjorie Caine, Kim Chambers, Mouse Choudhury, Charley Cook, Josh Cook, Caroline Crolla, Mari Cruice, Josh Dart, Jackie Devereaux, Patrick Donaghue, Claire Edmeades, Bruce Edwards, Linda Edwardes-Evans, Becky Ellers, Claire Ellison, Emma Exelby, Melanie Gadsby, Sarah Gammon, Theresa Gooda, Rebecca Griffiths, Lu Hales-Greer, Dick Hancock, Leo Hardt, Michelle Hayes, Ros Hoskins, Lisa Hostick, Sheelagh Hubbard, Cathy Hunt, Stephen Jacklin, Humainah Jameel, Debra Jewell, Esther Jillett, Judith Kneen, Sarah Lambert, Louise Lambourn, Matthew Lane, Morlette Lindsay, Geeta Ludhra, Katherine MacMahon, Lindsey Masters, Ian McEwen, Eleanor Milligan, Gill Munn, Emily Nell, Aoife Nolan, Lola O'Sullivan, Michele Otway, Laura Ovenden, Adam Parkhouse, Samantha Platt, Johnny Richmond, Jemma Rigby, Thomas Ripper, Lou Robbins-Ferreira, Robin Rudd, Daryl Slade, Cheryl Smith, Lorna Smith, Victoria Smith, Mark Steinhardt, Hannah Swain, Nicola Teasdale, Tessa Thomas, Helen Trelford, Vicki Tucker, Claire Twinn, Tracy Tyrell, Ian Usher, Claire Wapshare, Janet Ward, Chris Warren, Kim Wheeler, Meriel Whelan, John Wilks, Annette Williams.

Special thanks to Christine Cziko, Casey Daugherty and Richard Sterling, who have shared their experience with the project.

Chapter 1

Why teachers' writing groups?

> I have felt completely enriched by this project and very grateful to be part of it. From the beginning there has seemed to me to be two parts to this: improving ourselves as writers and increasing our awareness and effectiveness as teachers of writers. They do of course merge somewhere along the way.
>
> (Buckinghamshire teacher)

Teachers' writing groups are making a difference to the teaching of writing. They provide a place where teachers write and talk together in ways that enhance their individual practice as writers and as teachers of writing. Collectively, teachers work to understand, deepen and extend their practice and, in our experience, find pleasure in so doing. That those who teach writing should write is often asserted, but less frequently achieved (Emig 1983; Graves 1983; Andrews 2008; Andrews & Smith 2011). The groups that exist in the UK as part of what we have called the National Writing Project UK (NWP UK) have their roots in the National Writing Project USA (NWP USA) and in our personal experience of writing together over several decades.

To teach writing you need to be able to write

Writing is where all groups begin. The writing is not, in the first instance, writing in order to become a better teacher, but simply to experience the sheer pleasure of it; to find, however hesitant one may be, that we can all write and that we can find the forms and ways of writing that suit us best. We are likely to be surprised. We are likely to have moments of struggle and self-doubt, but above all, writing groups generate happiness.

> Writing makes people happy. One of the main features of the group is the enthusiasm and excitement with which we all meet up. I feel much happier after the meetings, and although the chat and banter are a part of this, the core is definitely that space that's provided to think and express myself in writing.
>
> (London teacher)

We have found that teachers who meet and write together gain particular understandings of the nature of writing. Their subsequent confidence and personal knowledge has a powerful effect in their classrooms. They also know that writing and sharing writing is of great personal value: emotionally and intellectually and in terms of professional identity. Their deepening understanding of the nature of writing for themselves, each other and for those whom they teach is one of the most powerful reasons for being part of a group.

In 2008 Richard Andrews made the case for a National Writing Project for teachers in the UK, identifying continuing concerns about the lower performance of young writers in comparison to performance in reading and consequent questions about the teaching of writing.

Andrews lists the basic tenets of the National Writing Project approach as follows:

1. To teach writing you need to be able to write.
2. Students should respond to each other's writing.
3. The teacher should act as writer alongside the students, and be prepared to undertake the same assignments as the students.
4. There is research about the teaching of writing that needs to be considered and applied, where appropriate, in the classroom.
5. Teachers can be their own researchers in the classroom.
6. The best teacher of writing is another writing teacher.
7. Various stages of the writing process need to be mapped and practised: these include pre-writing, drafting, revising, editing, conferencing (see no. 2 above) and publishing.

(Andrews 2008)

The proposal was well-supported by the experience of the NWP USA and showed clearly how a similar project might be developed in the UK. The idea is founded on a belief in the professionalism and authority of teachers and has the potential to be a powerful force for good.

Although funding was not secured, Simon Wrigley and Jenifer Smith initiated a number of grassroots projects which have led to the establishment of a network of teachers' writing groups across the country. Groups meet and operate in different ways. Many meet at the weekend in public spaces. Others have the luxury of a monthly meeting in a designated space. Most groups begin by establishing their own writing practices. The very fact that all group members are teachers or teaching assistants (TAs) means that teaching will soon enter any conversation and reflection. For many groups this has become a formal part of the session. This is where the principle of teachers teaching teachers begins.

Five core principles

The NWP USA website (www.nwp.org) lists five core principles which have informed our thinking about teachers' writing groups.

1. Teachers at every level, from early years on, are agents of reform. The US experience suggests that universities are ideal partners for investing in that reform through professional development. This is something that we need to develop.
2. In order to learn more about how we can best teach writing, we need to develop opportunities for professional development that help us to understand how writers develop, from pre-school to university and across the curriculum.
3. Knowledge about the teaching of writing is drawn from the interrelationship between theory and research, reflection on practice and the experience of writing. Teachers' writing groups can be informed by that triangular relationship: reading, teaching and writing.
4. There is no single right approach to teaching writing; however, as groups work together, they find that some practices prove to be more effective than others. The informed community of practice is in a strong position to develop thinking about the teaching of writing.
5. Teachers' writing groups can foster informed and authoritative practitioners who are well-placed to be teachers of other teachers and partners in educational research. Herein lies the potential for powerful educational reform.

Communities of practice

Teachers' writing groups offer the possibility of personal and professional autonomy. Through writing together and sharing pedagogy, teachers gain authority as teachers of writing. Whilst teachers do write for themselves without belonging to a group, a community of writers strengthens and extends learning. Together teachers discover and re-assert their knowledge as reflective classroom practitioners. The group creates a safe place where ideas and writing can be shared and where one can rely on a trusted audience. The strength of the safe space grows with the established community and makes creative risk-taking both within the group and in individual practice increasingly possible. Wenger's (1999) work provides a lens through which to consider the communities that are teachers' writing groups.

The established group is very often a community which crosses boundaries of age and experience, incorporating experienced teachers and those new to the profession and including teachers of early years through to those who teach A level. Each teacher brings with them their experience of the school and classroom where they work and of their experience of writing and teaching in different contexts. The writing group is the space where meanings are negotiated.

> [C]ommunities of practice are a privileged locus for the *acquisition* of knowledge . . . and . . . a good context to explore radically new insights without becoming fools or stuck in some dead end. A history of mutual engagement around a joint enterprise is an ideal context for this kind of leading-edge learning, which requires a strong bond of communal competence along with a deep respect for

the particularity of experience. When these conditions are in place, communities of practice are a privileged locus for the creation of knowledge.

(Wenger 1999: 214)

The secure environment of an established teachers' writing community fosters reflection and risk-taking. Individuals negotiate their own practice in relation to their school community and that of the writing group. Teachers are able to absorb new perspectives and make them part of their identity. Equally, they are able to bring to the group ways of thinking that provoke reflection and potential transformation.

Teachers' writing groups derive a particular energy from the writing/teaching dynamic. Teachers who engage in writing, responding, and reflecting on writing, imagine and negotiate new understandings of writing and the writing process. Simultaneously, they imagine and re-imagine their own and others' classrooms. The act of writing itself and of listening to writing is fundamental. It is both personal and social. The sharing of raw first drafts and the talk that surrounds them, have the potential to be transformative. Richard Andrews, who was a critical friend for the Buckinghamshire Teachers as Writers (TAW) group, affirmed that such a project gives teachers agency, translating personal knowledge into professional knowledge (personal communication).

Professional responsibility to self

We have a professional responsibility to ourselves. The group affirms that everyone's voice matters. When they join a teachers' writing group, teachers find a voice, both personal and professional. The writing group affords the opportunity to write in any way individuals wish, and to explore ideas, memories and ways of being that are important and authentic. Essentially, writing regularly, especially with a sympathetic but properly critical audience improves one's own writing. We hear our own words spoken and learn how others hear them. We are interested and challenged by what others choose to write and how they write. Writing often, improves writing. Writing with others adds a crucial dimension. Writing oneself gives the added knowledge and experience to the teaching of writing. Not only does one realise that many of our expectations for children's writing are unrealistic, more importantly one knows how different aspects of the writing process can be experienced. We have some knowledge of what might work and how to help young writers. It gives us confidence in ourselves as writers; we feel able to write alongside children when they write. It develops our repertoire of prompts and strategies. It gives us a language and a way of thinking. It allows us to be open to the surprise of what young writers bring. It strengthens our capacity to plan for possibility rather than prescribe outcomes.

Many of these benefits can come from writing alone and attending a regular writing group. Some of us belong to such groups, where the focus on our own craft is sharper. However the conversation about pedagogy is a distinctive feature of teachers' writing groups. Writing for ourselves within a community of teachers transforms our identities and contributes to the growth of that community.

One thing I really like about writing is that it makes you feel very connected with others. It's more than gratifying when your words touch someone else – it's imperative to human happiness to feel understood and know that, on whatever level, your words are listened to. I am consistently surprised by the unexpected connections I feel with other people's words – how much power we have as writers collectively. I am surprised by the fact that an activity which can seem so absolutely individual can actually reveal what makes us so similar to one another.

(Secondary teacher)

Professional responsibility to others

Teachers' writing groups are re-claiming, re-discovering and re-defining writing. They are taking responsibility for themselves as creative and thoughtful practitioners and recognising their professional responsibility to others. These groups respect the authority of the teacher at whatever stage in their career. Groups which include students and recently qualified teachers have a particular energy. They benefit from the range of experience and viewpoints and develop a deep understanding of what writing does and is, what it can do and what it is becoming. Teachers regularly share work from their own classrooms and welcome each other to visit their schools. They quickly see that everyone has something of value to teach others. They see their ideas spooling back to them through the work of others. They build the capacity to engage critically and knowledgeably with ideas and material. Their shared ideas and understandings are rendered trustworthy through critical dialogue and lived experience. In re-claiming the teaching of writing they are acquiring an authority that goes beyond the group.

Introducing teachers' writing groups

We hope to share some of what we have learned alongside the teachers whose voices you will hear as you read. We will share some of the principles and practice of setting up and being part of a teachers' writing group. We hope that you will feel encouraged to start a group yourself or at least to join a group. Through working together we are beginning to identify the areas which demand further classroom research, so this book is part handbook and part invitation to teacher researchers.

The book is designed so that teachers' voices are heard clearly throughout. It is also a starting point, a call for others to engage with, experiment, reflect and research in order to re-articulate what writing can be in schools and the pedagogies that will best support young writers.

I will always remember that weekend. I met a small group of fellow English teachers in a dusty, light-filled, Cambridge college room. . . . We looked at quirky objects and wandered among anthropological artefacts. I wrote about Kant and a pair of goggles; I wrote a narrative piece from the perspective of an ancient, female nude which ended with a mocking, shocking expletive. As I read my work to a supportive audience of strangers, I was genuinely surprised by what I had written. Words had come easily and ideas had slipped out, fully formed. It was my ugly duckling moment. For the first time in thirty-nine years, I saw myself as a writer. And it was thrilling.

I know that other people in the room were equally exhilarated by their experiences. Each of us seemed to have discovered and uncovered something of our*selves*. Throughout the sunlit, Cambridge day, we moved between the personal and the political, the playful and the philosophical. We explored our sense of empathy and held stones as if they were our children. We connected. Just connected.

[Six years] later, we still regularly meet. We rendezvous in stunning, London venues: Regent's Park; the British Museum; the steps of the V&A. We talk and write and then talk about our writing. It feels like a precious network of fellow travellers. Our group has broadened and our friendships have deepened. We have begun to post our work online and to discuss aspects of teaching and writing over the ether. We are a genuine community of practice.

(Secondary teacher, London Association of Teachers of English [LATE] Conference)

We encourage you to read this book in any order you like. Broadly, Chapters 1–10 focus on writing with teachers. Chapters 11–13 privilege teachers' words. Chapters 14–18 have a greater emphasis on classroom practice. Chapter 19 looks to the future and Chapter 20 provides an annotated book list.

References

Andrews, R. (2008) *The Case for a National Writing Project for Teachers*. Reading: CfBT Education Trust.

Andrews, R. & Smith, A. (2011) *Developing Writers: Teaching and Learning in the Digital Age*. Maidenhead: Open University Press.

Emig, J. (1983) *The Web of Meaning: Essays on Writing, Teaching, Learning, and Thinking*. Upper Montclair, NJ: Boynton/Cook.

Graves, D. (1983) *Writing: Teachers and Children at Work*. Portsmouth, NH: Heinemann Educational Books.

Wenger, E. (1999) *Communities of Practice*. Cambridge: CUP.

Chapter 2

Teachers' writing groups
A brief history

In 1966, twenty English educators were invited [and funded] to meet with colleagues from North America at Dartmouth College, Hanover, New Hampshire. The seminar represented the Modern Language Association, the National Council of Teachers of English and the National Association for the Teaching of English. They met because they were aware that the teaching of English was 'facing a series of critical problems and that an international exchange of experience and opinion would be helpful at arriving at solutions' (Dixon 1969). The month's seminar, despite its disagreements and cultural misunderstandings was, above all, remembered as a time of great excitement and was to influence English teaching for the decades that followed. John Dixon's account of the seminar acknowledges the impossibility of encapsulating all that was discussed and takes cognisance of what was not highlighted. In his chapter on teacher education he first mentions the value to teachers of experiencing for themselves all aspects of language use.

> [T]eachers of English at all levels should have more opportunities to enjoy and refresh themselves in their subject, using language in operation for all its central purposes. . . . Teachers without this experience – who would never think of writing a poem, flinch at the idea of 'acting', and rarely enter into discussion of the profounder human issues in everyday experience – are themselves deprived and are likely in turn to limit their experience of their pupils. On the other hand . . . just because language is so vital and pervading a concern, mature men and women can surprise themselves by the imaginative power they suddenly realise they possess, given the right opportunity.
>
> (Dixon 1969: 107)

Later in the same chapter he explores the relationship between school and university in the education of teachers and the possibility of creating 'a kind of intellectual community among college people and school people'. Such groups working together would decide on the important questions, create curricular materials and 'rethink these things for ourselves'.

This prompted Frank Whitehead (1970) to provide drama and creative writing sessions as part of a full-time course for in-service teachers at Sheffield University. Creative writing was particularly successful in persuading him that this should form a part of all in-service training for teachers.

> In what ways, then had we benefitted from our writing experience? First, as human beings we had gained the reassurance that our creative powers were still alive, in spite of long disuse; as an accompaniment to this it had once become open to us to use the medium of writing for our own purposes. . . . Secondly, as teachers we had gained an insight into the verbal creative process which it would have been impossible to acquire in any other way. I have no doubt that this will radically modify the attitude of each one of us towards the writing done by children . . .
>
> (Whitehead 1970: 82)

Whitehead's 'experiment' does not, despite its success, seem to have been replicated at the time.

The model of teachers writing together and sharing practice has been established in the United States of America since the early 1970s. The National Writing Project, which now has 200 university-based sites nationwide and beyond, began in the Bay Area of California. James Gray initiated, with others, the first 'summer institute', the Bay Area Writing Project (BAWP). The model created an environment where classroom teachers and professors of English and English education worked together in a way that celebrated classroom expertise. James Gray (2000) is refreshingly open about the mistakes and false starts of the early days of the project. It seems, even, that it was serendipity that the focus was writing, rather than mathematics. It was the model of professional development that was revolutionary in the first instance. The emphasis was on the sharing of practice through demonstration lessons and the vision that teachers can be agents of reform. That inclusive and mutually responsible approach to teacher development remains at the centre of the project. Its focus on writing and learning is significant.

The Summer Invitational Institute remains a cornerstone of the NWP USA alongside the very many other activities that the project now generates. A group of approximately fifteen to twenty teachers from all phases are invited to a four or five-week intensive 'learning community' hosted by a college or university. Participants write together, share their writing in response groups, and offer demonstrations of successful classroom practices from their own classrooms. When teachers share their practice through a workshop, it is they who determine its content and shape. This allows the project to remain open to new ideas and approaches.

> The writing project is not a writing curriculum or even a collection of best strategies; it is a structure that makes it possible for the exemplary teachers to share with other teachers ideas that work.
>
> (Gray 2000: 83–84)

Whitney and Friedrich's (2013) exploration of what they called the legacy of the NWP USA, that is, its lasting effects, identified three 'orientations of NWP teachers': towards writing, writers, and the teaching of writing. NWP teachers see writing as a tool for learning and the development of ideas and value these for their own sake. It means that they frame opportunities for students to develop ideas, say important things and develop their ability to say these effectively to audiences that matter. Whilst they value both fluency and form, they emphasise fluency before form in their work with students. Thinking about students as writers means that teachers make the teaching of process an explicit part of their work. They teach students a variety of ways to generate text, model processes themselves and are active and explicit in helping students to improve written texts. Finally, teachers link their teaching of writing to their own experience as writers.

> They then positioned themselves among students as a writer among writers, many times writing alongside the students. And they used their own ongoing experiences as writers to gain insight into the supports their students would need as they worked.
>
> (Whitney & Friedrich 2013)

Whitney and Friedrich found that NWP teachers' orientations transcended any particular set of lessons or strategies a teacher might use. Their teaching could not be summed up by describing a specific system. Whilst this made it difficult for the researchers to capture 'observable changes in classroom practice' it led them to understand the value of orientation within a view of professional development conceptualised as 'a decades-long series of encounters with ideas and strategies'. Orientations allow teachers to organise and synthesise the new knowledge and practice that they encounter over the course of their careers in a principled way. This finding is useful in thinking about how we can capture the impact of teachers' writing groups.

The findings of the Legacy Study and the Local Site Research Initiative (NWP 2008) show that participation in the NWP has an impact on retention, progression and personal development which is reflected in the classroom. The Local Site Research Initiative studies show significantly greater gains in students' writing achievement compared with classrooms where teachers had not participated in the NWP.

In an interview with Richard Andrews, Richard Sterling, Director of the NWP USA 1994–2008, observed:

> the added benefit that I think was hardly understood at the early days [of the project] is that when teachers start writing extensively, they discover things about themselves as learners that are almost an epiphany . . . the writing is at the centre, and they are writing all the time. I can only say to you it is one of the most powerful things they take from it; it engages them intellectually in their profession again. It's extraordinary to see and it happens every time . . .
>
> That's the heart of it, the personal engagement. . . . So writing is very important but it's not about turning them into creative writers, fiction writers, drama writers; that's not the point. The point is that the process of writing is a way to organise your thinking and your learning and also excite you about what you know yourself.
>
> (Andrews 2008: 37)

In 1985 a National Writing Project (NWP) was set up in England and Wales by the School Curriculum Development Committee later reconstituted as the National Curriculum Council. The project continued until 1989 and ran in about one quarter of the education authorities in those two countries. The project was set up at a time of radical change both in terms of government legislation and the influences of American theoretical knowledge of writing. Written language had received little attention since the Bullock Report (DES 1975) and the Schools Council Project: *The Development of Writing Abilities 11–18* (Britton *et al.* 1975). The aims of the project were characterised thus:

> to develop and extend the competence of children and young adults to write for a range of purposes and variety of audiences, in a manner that enhances their growth as individuals, their powers of self-expression, their skill as communicators and their facility as learners.
>
> (SCDC 1986 quoted in White 1991)

Teachers' writing groups were not part of the project's methodology, though teachers did write together, notably in Wiltshire under the leadership of Pat D'Arcy. What is significant in terms of this history is the way that the project was rooted in practice. A full range of schools and teachers were involved in the project which unlike the NWP USA did not target only centres of excellence. Teachers from different phases worked together, learning from each other and creating resources together. The project generated ideas and materials which remain of relevance today. However, its work was overtaken by the advent of the English National Curriculum and changes to the exam system. Although many NWP teachers gave evidence to the Kingman and Cox committees (White 1991), much that had been achieved was diluted in the years that followed. From 1989 onwards, 'English' became the focus of anxiety. It was, and still is, regarded as a national priority and so subject to all manner of interventions. Writing remains a subject in which children's test scores trail behind their scores in reading.

At about the same time, influenced by the American project, a National Writing Project was established in New Zealand which ran from 1987 to 1990. It was funded by the Department of Education with distinct projects based in four urban centres. No comprehensive and consistent research was implemented to measure the impact of the project on student writing however the conclusions of an informal evaluation (Carruthers & Scanlon 1990) are very similar to the findings of similar projects:

- as the teachers became writers themselves their attitude to the teaching of writing changed;
- how the teachers taught writing changed;
- student writing improved as a result of these changes; and
- teachers demonstrated their new skills and knowledge to other teachers.

Whilst there have been a number of projects in the UK in the last decade which involve teachers' writing, there is still no clear model of how these might develop. Teresa

Cremin's research with writing teachers has focused variously on 'creativity and writing' (Grainger *et al.* 2005), on uncertainty and discomfort (Cremin 2006) and on teachers' identities as writers (Cremin & Baker 2010). Cremin (2006: 432) suggests that 'the learning entitlement of teachers . . . should involve written composition at their own level'. The Writing is Primary project (Ings, undated) recognises the importance of leadership and whole school commitment. Although there is some suggestion that such a project is not for every teacher, there is also acknowledgement of the value of peer dissemination. The Teachers and TAs as Writers project, overseen by Jonathan Rooke, takes as its focus the kind of writing and writing practices that teachers might expect children to undertake in primary classrooms. The rationale for many UK teachers' writing groups has tended to emphasise craft knowledge and is less likely to characterise writing as a process that informs thinking and learning. Cremin and Myhill (2012), whilst valuing a consideration of 'one's compositional journeys and the social and affective nature of writing', have reservations about how effective writing teachers groups can be. They suggest that it is not easy to transform the subject knowledge acquired by teachers who write into pedagogic practice and draw attention to the need for more research in the area. It is undoubtedly true that further research is required.

Nevertheless, in 2008, in the light of the success of the NWP USA and a national concern about the standard of children's writing in England, Richard Andrews made a persuasive case for a National Writing Project for teachers (Andrews 2008), and despite failing to secure funding, continues to promote the idea. He modelled his proposal on the American Summer Institute, recommending that universities should provide the centre for such provision, linking closely to partner schools. This remains an ideal solution to developing such a project in the UK, though our own experience of writing groups might suggest some adaptations. Richard Andrews' proposal prompted others to action. Between 2009 and 2011 Terry Locke and his team at the University of Waikato (Locke *et al.* 2011) initiated a highly successful Teachers as Writers project which drew on the arguments marshalled by Andrews and was supported by an American NWP colleague. The New Zealand project had at its centre an intensive university-based course. Locke (2014) engaged with issues around the formulaic teaching of genre, placing an emphasis on composing, and explored the challenges of writing in the twenty-first century. This project also engaged head-on with rhetoric and teachers' varying subject knowledge. This New Zealand project affirms the power of teachers writing for themselves, especially in terms of confidence and self-efficacy. It raises the question of how teachers' writing groups can best be managed. Who is the authority?

At the same time, motivated by his own participation in writing groups, Simon Wrigley, at that time English Advisor for Buckinghamshire, took the decision to set up a writing project for teachers in the county, which became known as the Buckinghamshire TAW (Teachers As Writers) project. He worked in partnership with Jenifer Smith, through whom he had first experienced teachers' writing groups. Richard Andrews acted as a critical friend for the project and met regularly with participating teachers. The Buckinghamshire TAW group met over a period of four years. They wrote together and shared their writing both face-to-face and on a closed Virtual Learning Environment

(VLE). As Locke *et al.* (2011) found, sharing and responding to each other's writing had noted impact on practice (Andrews & Smith 2011; Smith & Wrigley 2012).

The TAW project followed a pattern that Jenifer Smith had developed since she first worked with Pat D'Arcy and then in Reflective Writing Workshops at National Association for the Teaching of English (NATE) conferences from 1990–1997. Simon attended the workshop in 1992 which was run by Jenifer with James Britton, Nancy Martin and Gordon Pradl. In that year, a writers' group was established, meeting for one weekend each term. It continues to do so. Jenifer has integrated writing into workshops in her role as advisory teacher in Suffolk and in her teaching pre- and in-service teachers at the University of East Anglia (UEA). She has run teachers' writing groups at UEA since 2002. The approach is one that is described in this book. Teachers write for themselves. They are encouraged to write reflectively as well as to experiment with a variety of forms. The talk that runs through any meeting combines reflection on writing and on teaching. Group members share their reading not only of poetry and prose but also theoretical and professional texts about writing and teaching writing. Teacher autonomy and professional responsibility towards the self and others is fundamental to the way groups are run.

In the same year that Buckinghamshire TAW was launched, Simon and Jenifer began running workshops together at the NATE conference. From these beginnings the NATE Writing Project has grown. It was established in 2009 (Wrigley & Smith 2010; Wrigley 2012). At the time of writing there is a network of about twenty grass-roots teachers' writing groups supported by the NWP website and through termly meetings of group leaders. Four of these groups have close links with university Schools of Education. Since 2009 we have presented at the NATE conference and at UKLA conferences. The London Association for the Teaching of English (LATE) organised a series of day conferences at The British Library and consequently generated further London-based groups. In 2013, Goldsmiths, University of London, launched an imaginative Writer/Teacher MA where 'practices of creative writing and of teaching and learning are brought into a productive relationship'. We have begun to make fruitful links with others who are passionate about writing and the teaching of writing, including the National Association of Writers in Education (NAWE) and the Arvon Foundation. This year we received news of the Maynooth Summer Institute for Teachers which was set up with teachers from the Bay Area Writing project in 2014. Their week long institute is very much modelled on the NWP USA example and the outcomes already report teachers' renewed energy and sense of agency. It is our aspiration to run longer residential institutes to support writing teachers in England.

This book goes some way towards explaining the work that we and many other teachers have done, not only to establish writing groups but to revisit the teaching of writing and to reshape pedagogy. We have been well supported by visitors from NWP USA who have shared their experience and joined meetings at local and national level and who have affirmed, in Richard Sterling's words, that the project has 'captured in spirit and substance the essence of what makes writing project work successful'. Teachers' writing groups are pleasurable for many reasons. The pleasure is personal in terms of one's own growth through writing, and professional, in that individuals are able to re-connect with the reasons that made them choose to become teachers. Teachers' writing groups strengthen professionalism and are drivers for change.

References

Andrews, R. (2008) *The Case for a National Writing Project for Teachers*. Reading: CfBT Education Trust.

Andrews, R. & Smith, A. (2011) *Developing Writers: Teaching and Learning in a Digital Age*. Maidenhead: Open University Press.

Britton, J., Burgess, T., Martin, N., McLeod. A. & Rosen, H. (1975) The Development of Writing Abilities (11–18). London: Macmillan.

Carruthers, A. & Scanlan, P. (1990) Report on the New Zealand Writing Project: An informal evaluation. *English in Aotearoa*, 11, 14–18.

Cremin, T. (2006) 'Creativity, uncertainty and discomfort: teachers as writers.' In *Cambridge Journal of Education*, 36(3), 415–433.

Cremin, T. & Baker, S. (2010) 'Exploring teacher-writer identities in the classroom: Conceptualising the struggle.' In *English Teaching: Practice and Critique*, Dec 2010, 9(3), 8–25.

Cremin, T. & Myhill, D. (2012) *Writing Voices Creating Communities of Writers*. Abingdon: Routledge.

DES: Department of Education and Science. (1975) *A language for life: report of the committee of inquiry appointed by the Secretary of State for Education and Science under the Chairmanship of Sir Alan Bullock*. London: HMSO.

Dixon, J. (1969) *Growth through English*. 2nd edn. Oxford: for NATE by Oxford University Press.

Grainger, T., Goouch, K. & Lambirth, A. (2005) *Creativity and Writing Developing Voice and Verve in the Classroom*. Abingdon: Routledge.

Gray, J. (2000) *Teachers at the Center: A Memoir of the Early Years of the National Writing Project*. Berkeley, CA: National Writing Project.

Ings, R. (undated) *Writing is Primary: Action Research on the Teaching of Writing in Primary Schools*. Esmee Fairbairn Foundation.

Locke, T. (2014) *Developing Writing Teachers: Practical Ways for Teacher-Writers to Transform their Classroom Practice*. London & New York: Routledge.

Locke, T., Whitehead, D., Dix, S. & Cawkwell, G. (2011) 'New Zealand teachers respond to the 'National Writing Project' experience.' In *Teacher Development*, 15(3), 273–291.

NWP (2008) *Local Site Research Initiative reports*. Retrieved from www.nwp.org/cs/public/download/nwp_file/12418/LSRI_CohortII&III_SummaryReport.pdf?x-r=pcfile_d

Smith, J. & Wrigley, S. (2012) 'What has writing ever done for us? The power of teachers' writing groups.' In *English in Education*, 46(1), Spring 2012, 70–84.

White, J. (1991) *Changing Practice: A History of the National Writing Project 1985–1989*. York: NCC.

Whitehead, F. (1970) *Creative Experiment: Writing and the Teacher*. London: Chatto & Windus.

Whitney, A. E. & Friedrich, L. (2013) 'Orientations for the Teaching of Writing: A Legacy of the National Writing Project.' In *Teachers College Record*, Volume 115, 070305, July 2013, 1–37.

Wrigley, S. (2012) 'The benefits of freedom.' In *NATE Classroom*, Spring 2012, 11–14.

Wrigley, S. & Smith, J. (2010) 'Making Room for Writing: The NATE Writing project.' In *English Drama Media*, October 2010, 13–19.

Chapter 3

Approaching writing and writing teachers

Writing makes you think about words in a responsible way.

(Teacher educator)

Teachers' writing groups in the UK approach writing and its teaching in ways that are fluid, open, exploratory and celebratory. The tenets of the National Writing Project outlined by Andrews (2008) – listed in Chapter 1 – provide a structure which parallels the NWP as it is practiced in the US. This approach draws on the actual experience of teachers writing whether alone or in the company of good writing friends. It captures what they learn through teaching children of all ages and by working with other teachers both in the classroom and as part of professional development. Teachers continue to develop practices which, above all, honour the agency of the individual and the group. Understanding that even the very youngest writer learns best when they have charge of their own writing is fundamental to this approach. In addition, viewing teachers as agents of reform and as significant providers of mutual professional development shifts the centre of gravity in teaching practice. A shared and evolving development of understanding replaces the pre-packaged, delivered curriculum and encourages teacher innovation and decision-making. In teachers' writing groups teachers reconstruct and reclaim ownership of the craft. They engage in a dynamic process rooted in conversation with adults and children jointly engaged in the work of writing.

As teachers' writing groups form, get to know and trust each other, and settle into localised routines, key questions emerge. The questions are important. The writing group is an essential platform from which research into writing and teaching now should spring. Openness and trust are crucial; and a willingness to try things. Equally important is time and affirmation. Adult writers, especially, have decades of baggage to shed and we can never know, immediately, how writers will develop. Writers' preferences can differ and may reflect patterns of language use more generally. Sharples (1999) quotes Ali Wyllie's study of student and academic writers, which characterised writers in five ways: watercolourist, architect, bricklayer, sketcher and oil painter, which teacher-writers have found useful. He also suggests two categories – discoverers and planners – which echo, for example, Zadie Smith's (2011) 'Micro Managers' and 'Macro Planners'. Smith is a self-confessed Micro Manager:

> I start at the first sentence of a novel and I finish at the last. It would never occur to me to choose among three different endings because I haven't the slightest idea of the ending until I get to it, a fact that will surprise no one who has read my novels. Macro Planners have their houses largely built from day one, and so their obsession is internal – they're forever moving the furniture. They'll put a chair in the bedroom, the lounge, the kitchen and then back in the bedroom again. Micro Managers build a house floor by floor, discretely and in its entirety. Each floor needs to be sturdy and fully decorated with all the furniture in place before the next is built on top of it. There's wallpaper in the hall even if the stairs lead nowhere at all.
>
> Because Micro Managers have no grand plan, their novels exist only in the present moment, in a sensibility, in the novel's tonal frequency line by line.

Micro Managers sound remarkably like many young writers for whom writing narrative is a form of play. However carefully they have planned a story, the writing will take them in a different direction. That may be the nature of fiction. Other writing tasks will be approached differently depending on demands of audience, purpose, medium and content. However infuriating this may be to some teachers, we need to embrace the complexity and variety of writing, to acknowledge that it is 'cognitively expensive' (Myhill *et al.* 2008) and to accept that there is not a single system that will miraculously raise standards.

Writing teachers' groups can provide the focus for the study of writing from both inside–out and outside–in. The group itself is important. The community of writers is of the essence. Meetings are not simply about writing but about who we are as people and as teachers. A teachers' writing group works in opposition to the reification of writing as a set of skills and creates its own cultural and ideological space. Sharples (1999) suggests that writing is always in conversation, even if the conversation is only with oneself.

> All writing is collaborative. It has to be. Writers are in constant dialogue with the surrounding world and that world includes other people. Guidance from a teacher, support from a partner, criticism from a reader, a letter from a friend, a conversation in a bar can all alter the course of writing by offering ideas and constraints. The influences may be subtle but they are nonetheless direct.
>
> (Sharples 1999: 168)

In that sense writing groups provide a context for the teaching/writing conversation. Writing and sharing writing with others and the talk about the processes of writing and of teaching writing that ensues sit at the centre.

Writing practices in the classroom derive from the teacher's conceptual frameworks which provide the foundation for action. Those foundations can be strengthened and maintained by the community of writing teachers. When asked the question: 'In what ways do you think membership of the group has had an impact on your teaching of writing?' most teachers mentioned their strengthened confidence. This professional confidence comes from writing and talking with others, from developing subject knowledge and, we would argue, the time for personal reflection that a group affords. The confidence that teachers speak of derives from the co-operative. There is no specific formula. Every voice is heard. The writing group provides a model and a site for experimentation. From this an assured authority grows. It is the assured authority that we aspire to for those we teach, not a method, and so we each learn from our own experience, from our group and from our knowledge of and encounters with children. Michael Armstrong (2006) suggests that companionship was fundamental to the classrooms where the young writers whose stories he analyses were nurtured. The companionable classroom is not passive and the teacher's task, though pleasurable, is demanding. It requires knowledge of the child and the community, and a knowledge of writing.

The teachers' writing group begins with teachers writing for themselves. Other knowledge will follow. Most adults begin tentatively and their uncertainties must be acknowledged. The demands of both writing and teaching are great. We need to be both sensitive and robust. We need to create contexts where there is warmth, mutual respect, patience and openness; where there is a willingness to truly listen, to be silent as much as to be ready to speak. Well-being is important. We have a moral responsibility to others which is exercised through careful listening both to oneself and to others. The teachers' writing group does not model a school classroom in the sense that we do not specifically undertake tasks children might do but it does embody the values and principles we are likely to apply to teaching. Early in writing group membership and when some ideas are introduced to classrooms, the idea of permission arises. Emma Beynon (2014) coins the phrase 'pedagogy of permission'. Her invigorating account of how teachers and pupils were able to re-engage with writing through the Bath Festival's Write Team programme is very familiar to us. In their conclusion to *Making Poetry Happen* Wilson *et al.* (2014) make the case for a 'broader cultural vision, a more creative, artistic and engaged approach' (to poetry) that chimes well with the NWP approach to writing. Poetry affords very particular possibilities and we celebrate those:

> ideals of education which poetry so readily promotes (and at such little cost): community, confidence, creativity, identity, empathy, permission and sharing. Poetry resists teaching to prescribed objectives, as it resists atomistic approaches to assessment. Yet, as writer after writer in this book patiently sets out, far from being an 'escape from reality', poetry can provide us with some of our realest, most deeply felt and unexpected experiences. In the words of Jennie Clark, reading and writing poetry can and does 'help make a healthy, responsive, aware human being'.
>
> (Wilson *et al.* 2014: 201)

Permissions are needed, very often, because of the experiences of teachers and children in the context of high-stakes accountability (Sainsbury 2009) where writing is prescribed and the emphasis is on the outcome and not on the individual. It feels strange to be giving permission to colleagues, and perhaps what we do is simply affirm that it is OK to play, to experiment, to leave writing incomplete and to write about what is important to you.

In the beginning, for adults, what is important is likely to be personal. This sometimes comes as a surprise to the writer. Sometimes it can inhibit writing. Be patient. Writing about the self is never compulsory or even expected. Writing may not be autobiographical in the sense of a life narrative, but may be visible in terms of major preoccupations. One teacher, writing in London galleries, returned repeatedly to themes of feminism and textiles partly prompted by the context but more surely relating to ideas that were important to her. For others, writing serves other purposes. It is for the writer to discover what is important to them. We should not underestimate the power of expressive writing and suggest that it is the starting point for almost all writing. And that all writing may contain an element of expressive writing (Andrews & Smith 2011).

> We hold our conviction that the quality of learning could be improved if fuller use were made of the heuristic potential of expressive writing. The alternative hypothesis to which teachers must be working might be phrased as follows: "If you limp around long enough in somebody else's language you may eventually learn to walk in it."
>
> (James Britton in Pradl 1982)

In the Buckinghamshire group, one teacher's phrase 'to inhabit my life more fully' summed up for many what writing had done for them. Just as one notices the world more acutely if one begins to draw regularly, so writing sharpens perceptions. Through writing, teachers arrive at a sense of themselves that directly and indirectly will inform their teaching: writing and the shaping of self, journeying in (the reflective self), out (sharing with others), back (into memory) and forward (speculatively). They are also reclaiming the power of writing to learn (Britton in Pradl 1982; D'Arcy 1989; Mayher et al. 1983).

Thinking through writing seems to have been lost in the drive to teach pupils through a strict adherence to genre and the imperative to write to measurable criteria. Mitchell (2010) reminds us that university teachers are looking for 'something that reveals more of how the student is thinking and making sense of the new things they are learning'. Young writers, of whatever age, are in danger of never knowing what writing can afford them. We need to find a way of bringing the whole person into the writing equation, recognising the need for robust subject knowledge.

> The project to enfranchise children by revealing the rules and creating a 'culture of transparency' may enable them to pass examinations and lead to widening access. But it would be legitimate, in my view, to be concerned that this project could falter if it does not recognise that writing also functions for thinking, for making, and for developing self-identity, and that these kinds of writing contribute to full participation through literacy.
>
> (Mitchell 2010: 146)

The subject knowledge that the writing teacher needs to call upon is extensive and varied (Myhill *et al.* 2008). It needs to be remembered that whilst increased knowledge of grammar and 'the applied understanding of linguistics in written contexts' has its place, the teacher who writes is able to bring a fuller understanding of writing to their practice.

> Since joining the group, the respect I have for children as writers has increased. Often, in school, they have to write when they might not feel like it or don't have the confidence. I try to keep this in mind every time I suggest writing or set a writing task. I always ask children if they are happy for me to look at their writing, rather than just barge in and start reading. I'm not sure I would choose to attend a writing group if everything I wrote was up for external scrutiny. I am much more conscious of trying to find out what children think about their own writing than of passing my own judgement on their work or simply giving lots of praise.
>
> (Secondary teacher)

> Most importantly, I have the confidence to give students the creative space to explore their own writing. I respond more on a personal level, less on a 'right and wrong' basis. It's helped me get into the head of whoever's writing I'm reading, whether it's a child in my class or another adult.
>
> (Secondary teacher)

Armstrong (2006) emphasises the teacher's 'privilege' to create the context for children's writing and to interpret and respond to it in responsible ways. This relates to what happens in groups and the ways in which teachers think about teaching writing. All the elements of the writing classroom are present in teachers' writing groups and are reflected in the chapters of this book. Teachers think about contexts for writing, about the reading that informs and inspires writing, about writing for a known audience, the sharing of writing and responses to it, talk before, after and during writing, the uses of language, an attention to words and to grammar, the sources of inspiration for writing and the demands of different forms and media. They think about these things and more, because they all relate to their own writing as much as they do to the writing of those they teach. Our approach is to engage with our concerns as writers and to engage also with the concerns about teaching writing that are brought to meetings.

Whilst talk must give way to writing, and you are likely to listen more than you write, the interplay between talk and writing is crucial to the teachers' writing group where writing and talk work together in shaping ideas and in realising the self. Here, a Newly Qualified Teacher (NQT) reflects on the role that the group plays in her growing understanding of herself as a teacher of English:

> And what of that? Success? No. Progress? Probably. But perhaps in a broader sense than I'd originally envisioned. Certainly, there have been ideas I have pinched after our sessions and gone back and used within my classroom, some of which have

'worked', in the sense that students have bought in and produced some pieces they've felt really pleased with, some of which have been much harder to call. But, in all honesty, these have seemed (to date) like fairly ad-hoc additions to my teaching practice, rather than well-structured, more strategic adjustments (though this may have as much to do with the fact that I am an NQT in not the easiest of schools). Instead (or as well, depending on your glass-half- perspective), what I have noticed developing is my sense of who and what I want to be as a practitioner, and when and where and how I might achieve it. I suppose, if I wanted to be grand about it, I could say that my 'philosophy' of teaching English as a whole has grown.

And this, I think, must be directly attributed to the members of the group – both new and old – who I do genuinely think offer such inspiration, whether that be through their writing (which so often just amazes me), their conversation, or their exploits in the world beyond the group (or lunches after it) – be they activism or academia, making music or making cardigans.

Teachers' writing groups provide the opportunity for teachers to continue to grow; to establish their teaching identities within a trusted community; to take responsibility for and ownership of their professional practice.

I have noticed that the process of reflecting on our own writing, and that of the children or students we teach, develops our capacity to seamlessly move from our given intuitive understandings about writing to the frankly theoretical. Within the course of a few meetings, we begin to develop a sense of agency and confidence about writing; speak with a marked authority and are hungry for reading and dis-cussion. There is a growing commitment to professional enquiry and the construc-tion of theories of writing. It is of little surprise that many of our writing teachers naturally turn to research to legitimise these powerful theoretical constructs which have arisen from membership of a teachers' writing group.

(Teacher educator)

References

Andrews, R. & Smith, A. (2011) *Developing Writers: Teaching and Learning in the Digital Age*. Maidenhead: Open University Press.

Armstrong, M. (2006) *Children Writing Stories*. Maidenhead: Open University Press.

Beynon, E. (2014) in Dymoke, S., Barrs, M., Lambirth, A. & Wilson, A. (eds.) (2014) *Making Poetry Happen: Transforming the Poetry Classroom*. London: Bloomsbury Academic.

D'Arcy, P. (1989) *Making Sense, Shaping Meaning: Writing in the Context of a Capacity-based Approach to Learning*. Ports, NH: Boynton/Cook.

Mayher, J. S., Lester, N. & Pradl, G. M. (1983) *Learning to Write; Writing to Learn*. Portsmouth, NH: Boynton/Cook.

Mitchell, S. (2010) 'Now you don't see it; now you do. Writing made visible in the university.' In *Arts and Humanities in Higher Education*, 9(2), 133–148.

Myhill, D., Fisher, R., Jones, S., Lines, H. & Hicks, A. (2008) *Effective Ways of Teaching Com-plex Expression in Writing Research: A Literature Review of Evidence from the Secondary School Phase*. University of Exeter: Report DCSF-RR032.

Pradl, G. M. (ed.) (1982) *Prospect and Retrospect: Selected Essays of James Britton.* Montclair, NJ: Boynton/Cook.

Sainsbury, M. (2009) 'Developing writing in a high-stakes environment.' In Beard, R., Myhill, D., Riley, J. & Nystrand, M. (eds.) (2009) *The Sage Handbook of Writing Development.* London: Sage, pp. 213 231.

Sharples, M. (1999) *How We Write Writing as Creative Design.* London: Routledge.

Smith, Z. (2011) *Changing My Mind: Occasional Essays.* London: Hamish Hamilton.

Wilson, A. *et al.* (2014) in Dymoke, S., Barrs, M., Lambirth, A. & Wilson, A. (eds.) (2014) *Making Poetry Happen: Transforming the Poetry Classroom.* London: Bloomsbury Academic.

Chapter 4

Composing

Talking about the process is important. One of the first things that we found with the group, is that people wanted to discuss the process that they'd gone through in order to produce the writing. This never fails to be interesting, but more than that, it's taught me that the traditional planning techniques that I've taught in the classroom are far removed from this approach, and rather than inspiring writing, often seek to confine and sterilize it.

(Secondary teacher)

The discovery of a mismatch between what one teaches and how one approaches writing oneself is a common occurrence and the focus of many writing group conversations. It leads us to rethink classroom practices and to raise questions about assumptions we make about writing processes. Our collective experience of teaching across the age range affirms our understanding that our own writing practices may be different from those of a much younger writer only in terms of experience and maturity. We propose that, as in any cultural activity, there is a common thread that runs between the child writer and the adult writer and that the child, increasingly, acts and thinks in ways that the adult writer may do. Our awareness of our own writing practices informs our thinking as we encounter the child writer who constantly teaches us more about becoming a writer.

An understanding of composing is a key area for further research. It is part of the dynamic of the writing group that teachers' experience of and engagement with writing comes first and then the return to the classroom where assumptions and practices are reappraised and brought to the group for consideration. In writing this book, we have returned to the roots of our own thinking. We began with Pat D'Arcy in the 1970s, when she was part of the Schools Council's 'Writing Across the Curriculum' project and in the 1980s through her work with Wiltshire teachers. She introduced the thinking of key American writing teachers (Graves 1983; Emig 1983; Murray 1982; Fulwiler 1987; Mayher *et al.* 1983) through the NATE conferences of the time and through working closely with James Britton and Nancy Martin. It is through her and our conversations with them that this project has grown. It is timely to reappraise our thinking about the processes of writing and how these relate to pedagogy.

We understand writing to be dynamic, recursive, non-linear, hard to contain. Andrews and Smith (2011) suggest that writing could be compared to a large educational conference, seemingly chaotic but holding still discernible patterns of movement, constructs, decision-making. It is perhaps the fluid, indeterminate, shifting nature of writing that makes some people want to box it up. We understand that individuals find different approaches that work for them and thus strict directives are not always helpful. Holding those differences in the classroom is the difficult job of the teacher and why writing groups can be so empowering. Writing calls upon linguistic, cognitive, experiential, affective and motor skills. It involves everything working together in different configurations according to what is being written, by whom and why. It is difficult to disentangle the elements of writing and then put them back together. Pat D'Arcy (1989) suggests one way of categorising some of these elements:

- Writing as code: letters, words, sentences, spelling, punctuation, grammar, syntax.
- Writing as medium: handwriting, messy, neat, jotting down, playing around, shaping visible works, choosing chalk, pen or keyboard; the importance of play and exploration, the interplay of movement, visual image and alphabetic codes.
- Writing as product: list, poem, story, textbook, essay, article, letter. We need to remember that this takes time and that the product derives from the active process of shaping meaning and discovering what we have to say.
- Writing as active process: D'Arcy sees this as a process of discovery and rediscovery, 'a powerful means of attracting into consciousness retained experience that has already undergone some reprocessing in the inner recesses of the mind'. (p 23)

The teacher is required to keep all those many elements in mind as they create the conditions for children to become writers. We recognise the significance of learning the code and handling the medium and will return to that, but will first consider writing as an active process and how that sits in relation to composing. Andrews and Smith (2011) suggest that learning to write is learning to compose, placing the emphasis on process rather than the recent preoccupation with product.

This is a helpful shift and leads Andrews and Smith to develop their argument in favour of writing as design. We would like first to maintain steadier focus on the dynamic of writing. We are cautious about the sense of premeditation implied in 'design' and want to consider writing as invention and to remind ourselves of what writing brings as a way of learning. In an interview with John Mayher, James Britton explains how it can be useful to think of writing as spontaneous, more like speech, shaping at the point of utterance. The social pressures of a conversation, he suggests, can mean that the speaker arrives at solutions to problems that they have been unable to solve by simply thinking about them.

JOHN MAYHER: In other words, if writing is made too deliberate a process, you don't think it works?

JAMES BRITTON: Right, I think that spontaneity is an important part of invention and invention is what makes writing a means of learning.
(Mayher *et al.* 1983: 41)

It is our experience that there is a kind of writing that is shaped in the moment. It is often this kind of writing that reconnects teachers with what writing can do. It is writing that gives shape to experience and which taps into ideas and feelings that are important to us. It may be shaped later.

The notion that authoring involves getting ready-made thoughts onto paper is present in the 2014 National Curriculum for English and was the main thrust of the writing textbooks which are challenged in the work of Emig (1983) and Berthoff (1981). The idea of writing down a fixed idea is commonplace and yet when faced with the blank paper or screen would-be writers can be so overwhelmed they do not start to write, or they find their words running away with them and previously unshaped ideas appearing on the page (Elbow 1981). Barton (1994) acknowledges the significance that writing as process has, both from the student's and the teacher's point of view. The meta-cognitive awareness that derives from reflecting on writing processes contributes to the ways we choose to act in order to consolidate or to change what we do. This understanding of the nature and affordances of writing seem to us to be crucial in terms of developing writing teachers. It is not a method.

We have been cautious about how we conceptualise writing processes. Cremin and Myhill (2012) draw attention to critiques of process writing as a teaching method, though the critics they cite, Smith and Elley (1998) and Beard (2000), hold no greater credibility than they claim for Graves (1983) and his contemporaries. For some reason, they emphasise Lensmire's (1994) disillusion with what he describes as the Romanticism of Graves' approach, although his conclusions lead him to propose that 'teacher response to children's texts be *critically pragmatic*, and aimed at promoting an *engaged, pluralistic classroom community*' which seems entirely useful. It is possibly true that Graves (1983), Calkins (1983, 1994) and Murray (1982) report only 'success stories' (Cremin & Myhill 2012), but that is the danger of any proposal for teaching, whatever the line of thinking. The other danger is what Andrews and Smith (2011) describe as the narrowing of ideas that come with their mass production. In England, writing process became reified within the National Curriculum as planning, drafting, revising, editing, publishing. Process becomes taught as content. We seem to have lost touch with what the process looks like. Even though we often crave a simple structure, we have to remember that models are simply attempts to articulate processes and not the experience itself. In a writing teachers' group there is time to keep in touch with process and to think about our experience of this in relation to our experience of young writers.

Models of writing process (Berthoff 1981; Clark & Ivanic 1997; Sharples 1999; Mayher *et al.* 1983; Andrews & Smith 2010) attempt, on the two-dimensional page, to resist linearity and to encapsulate its three- and four-dimensional qualities. We have always liked the fluidity of 'percolating' (Mayher *et al.* 1983) and acknowledge that each text in its context demands different aspects of the process.

> *Percolating* involves everything that happens to the writer apart from the actual setting of marks on paper. . . . Percolating involves incubating, contemplating, or

rehearsing the experiences and ideas to be expressed in writing. Through percolating the writer begins to discover what she wants to say.

(Mayher *et al.* 1983: 5)

The most elegant model is that of Berthoff's double helix where three concepts of mind *opposing, naming, defining*, run up and down the spirals and work with each other in different configurations. Berthoff (1981) suggests that the composing process, forming/thinking/writing is one in which everything happens simultaneously. This dynamic, three-part characterisation of process parallels Murray's *pre-writing, writing, re-writing*. It seems a good place to start.

Berthoff emphasises the meaning-making affordances of writing. The double helix models the dialogues that take place within the writer's head and which can be enacted within the writing community. She suggests that, in writing, we make meanings from the chaos that surrounds us, that students can 'find their way out of the chaos' by learning its uses, by 'rediscovering the power of language to generate the sources of meaning'.

> I believe we can best teach the composing process by conceiving of it as a continuum of making meaning, by seeing writing as analogous to all those processes by which we make sense of the world. . . . Meanings don't just happen: we make them; we find and form them. . . . Learning to write is learning to do deliberately and methodically with words on the page what we do all the time with language.
>
> (Berthoff 1981: 69)

If students are to learn to write, Berthoff argues, to discover what language can do, then we must 'give them back their language, and that means playing with it, working with it, using it instrumentally, making many starts'. We would argue, that adults, also, need to reclaim the language that is their own. The playfulness and improvisational quality of much writing in teachers' writing groups is as important as anything else they might do.

Writers, and especially teachers of writing must be able to tolerate ambiguity and to live with indeterminacy. Why? Because, as Emig (1983) suggests, writing is *not* learned atomistically. Writers of all ages as frequently work from wholes to parts as from parts to wholes and there is a complex interplay between focal and global concerns. There is *not* one process of writing that fits all for every kind of writing, there are processes of writing that differ because of aim, purpose, context or audience and although some features are shared amongst writers, there are those that are individual, even idiosyncratic and these are to be celebrated and shared. Writing is *not* linear, entirely conscious and easily done to order. Writing is recursive and sometimes wandering. It is as often concerned with dreaming and composting as it is with careful planning and rendering. Teachers writing together experience this variety in their own writing and in hearing about the writing processes of others. And this is of value, because, for the most part, their classes contain thirty or so young writers in all their variety.

The process of writing can be enhanced by working in, and with, a group of other writers, perhaps especially a teacher, who give vital response, including advice.

(Emig 1983: 141)

Not only do we experience the strength of this in writing teachers' groups but we learn in fundamental ways how this can be replicated in our own classrooms.

Two studies by the research teams of Flower and Hayes, and Bereiter and Scardamalia are frequently cited seminal works in the cognitive approach to writing. Andrews and Smith (2010) provide a very useful overview and comparison of these which we recommend. Both teams compared the writing processes of children with those of adult writers. The two models are different and provoke different questions. Flower and Hayes developed a model with its layers and dynamics as one of competent writers' processes. Three sub-processes identified – planning, translating and reviewing – could be compared with Murray's *pre-writing, writing, re-writing* (Murray 1982). Older writers were found to move between processes with greater ease and seemed more able to orchestrate cognitive processes than younger writers. Bereiter and Scardamalia (1987) identified two distinct writing processes: knowledge-telling and knowledge transforming. Essentially the first is considered the simpler of the two processes, more likely, but not exclusively, to be used by children and is regarded as a kind of unproblematic setting down of ideas following a chain of mental associations; the second involves problem-solving and goal setting in terms of the writer's understanding of the writing task. It is considered a more deliberate conscious activity where the emerging text is modified in relation to what is written.

Broadly, this would seem to suggest that a child's capacity to manage the multiple elements of a writing task grows with maturity. However, whilst these studies are useful they may not be the most helpful lens through which to consider the writing of young children. Unsurprisingly, considerations of writing processes give little sense of the variety of writing tasks that might be undertaken and how this might change the way writing happens. This seems to us to be a rich opportunity for teachers' writing groups. Teachers writing together are able to use their growing awareness and understandings of their own writing processes and use that as a lens through which to view what children do in their classes. Very often we strictly frame children's writing in ways that prevent us from seeing what they can actually do and how they think so we should take opportunities to read and reflect on children's writing in order to better understand the ways in which children solve the problems that their writing sets for them.

Andrews and Smith (2011) argue that an emphasis on composing rather than writing relieves the pressure on writing as 'a medium of instruction and a system to be learnt'. They suggest that the idea of composition extends the scope of writing, and allows us to see it more surely as a multimodal medium more readily aligned with acts of composition in fields such as music, engineering and architecture. This move to position writing in this way, in terms of both the arts and sciences is full of possibility. It is also a response to the rapid changes in modes of communication in a digital age. Sharples (1999) arrived at a model for writing as design which also relates to Murray's *pre-writing, writing, re-writing* and emphasises the cyclical nature of writing, the opportunity for a dual flow of activity. Sharples calls upon rhetoric, literary theory and cognitive psychology in his endeavour to arrive at a 'design language' for writing. His chief requirement is that it should match the cycle of reflection and engagement which he suggests is fundamental to the writing process. Here are some Year 6 children thinking about process:

> I had a very interesting discussion with my Year 6 class just prior to the Easter break about the effectiveness of planning in relation to the writing process. We had just watched the YouTube video of Peter Elbow, during which the vast majority of the class, without prompting, wrote copious notes. The video ended and I was besieged with a sea of anxiously waving hands. "Mr S, I agree with him. I find planning really hard." Now, bearing in mind that this was top set year 6, this came as a mild revelation to me. Many of the children were of a similar opinion to Peter Elbow that planning for writing and the writing itself were completely different universes. Most children didn't look back at their plan once they started writing: "There's no point because you go off in different directions and then the plan becomes irrelevant," said one level 6 child. Some discarded the planning format and wrote a list of key words. Others, in an activity reminiscent of free writing, just wrote down ideas generated by the prompt – 'making a mess'. The discussion inevitably moved to the relevance of these findings in the light of the impending SATs tests. We discussed the two processes that Peter Elbow identifies in writing; the process of opening the door to creativity and the process of using the critical muscle to organise these thoughts and ideas. The planning time given in a SATs test, many believed, should be used for making a mess, opening the door, free writing of ideas and creative thinking. The remainder of the test would then employ the critical process to varying degrees as those ideas are put down on paper. Finally, it was agreed that during the last 5 minutes of the test, the critical muscle should reign supreme as checks are made for punctuation and grammar errors. It was interesting that so many children rebelled against the constraints of a plan, preferring the free writing that Peter Elbow advocates. I wonder what the implications of this are for teaching writing and, in particular, responding to the written SATs tests with their prescriptive planning formats?
>
> (Year 6 teacher)

Writing remains a way of making sense of experience. We learn through the act of writing. It would be a pity to lose the sense of writing as organic, exploratory, muscular. That first expressive urge for writing is often what hooks us. We need also the skills and understanding that work with the clay, the granite block in order to shape it. The current fashion for writing as design (Andrews & Smith 2011; Cremin & Myhill 2012) draws attention to decisions about sound, colour, image and the comparative importance of visual and written elements of any given composition. Very often, when the visual is prioritised, the written word takes on a different purpose though that is not true for young writers. The potential immediacy and scope of a digital readership and the possibility of writing in ways that are more surely rooted in young writers' cultures are issues that go well beyond writing as design. Perhaps that phrase is too limited? Our tentative understanding of design in the context of multimodality is that writing or writing practices, is/are one mode amongst many. A choice is to be made by the writer/designer – is writer the appropriate term? – amongst a wide range of modes according to purpose, audience and cultural context. What this means in practice needs thinking about. How near are we, as Gunther Kress asks, (Larson & Marsh 2015) to announcing the death of the paragraph and celebrating the triumph of the bullet-point list? There are discussions to be had amongst writing teachers who may be creating blogs, novels, stand-up routines, poetry, gaming scripts, multi-skilled fire performances.

Writing groups are learning to look more closely at the ways in which writing for children is both multimodal and shaped at the point of utterance. Writing for the very young writer is integral to movement, speech, drawing, drama, puppetry and more. It may be that we should be looking more closely at how we engage with multimodal texts and decision-making; that we need to articulate more clearly how these considerations inform our understanding of writing. When thinking about writing processes we need to be able to live with multiplicity. We can learn from the youngest writers and the most experienced. It will be an interesting project.

References

Andrews, R. & Smith, A. (2011) *Developing Writers: Teaching and Learning in the Digital Age.* Maidenhead: Open University Press.

Barton, D. (1994) *Literacy: An Introduction to the Ecology of Written Language.* Oxford: Blackwell Publishers.

Beard, R. (2000) *Developing Writing 3–13.* London: Hodder & Stoughton.

Bereiter, C. & Scardamalia, M. (1987) *The Psychology of Written Composition.* Hillsdale, NJ: Lawrence Erlbaum Associates, Inc.

Berthoff, A. (1981) *The Making of Meaning: Metaphors, Models and Maxims for Writing Teachers.* Upper Montclair, NJ: Boynton/Cook.

Calkins, L, M. (1983) *Lessons from a Child: On the Teaching and Learning of Writing.* Exeter, NH: Heinemann Educational Books.

Calkins, L.M. (1994) *The Art of Teaching Writing.* 2nd Ed. Portsmouth, NH: Heinemann.

Clark, R. & Ivanic, R. (1997) *The Politics of Writing.* Abingdon: Routledge.

Cremin, T. & Myhill, D. (2012) *Writing Voices Creating Communities of* Writers. Abingdon: Routledge.

D'Arcy, P. (1989) *Making Sense, Shaping Meaning: Writing in the Context of a Capacity-based Approach to Learning.* Ports, NH: Boynton/Cook.

Elbow, P. (1981) *Writing with Power: Techniques for Mastering the Writing Process.* New York, Oxford: Oxford University Press.

Emig, J. (1983) *The Web of Meaning: Essays on Writing, Teaching, Learning, and Thinking.* Upper Montclair, NJ: Boynton/Cook.

Fulwiler, T. ed., (1987) *The Journal Book.* Portsmouth, NH: Boynton/Cook.

Graves, D. (1983) *Writing: Teachers and Children at Work.* Portsmouth, NH: Heinemann Educational Books.

Larson, J. & Marsh, J. (2015) *Making Literacy Real: Theories and Practices for Learning and Teaching.* London: Sage Publications.

Lensmire, T. J. (1994) *When Children Write: Critical Re-visions of the Writing Workshop.* New York, NY: Teachers College Press.

Mayher, J. S., Lester, N. & Pradl, G. M. (1983) *Learning to Write; Writing to Learn.* Portsmouth, NH: Boynton/Cook.

Murray, D. M. (1982) *Learning by Teaching.* Montclair NJ: Boynton Cook.

Sharples, M. (1999) *How We Write: Writing as Creative Design.* London: Routledge.

Smith, J. & Elley, W. (1998) *How Children Learn to Write.* London: Longman.

Chapter 5

Writing histories

In my travels around classrooms I'd see the fundamental problem as not one of proficiency but in terms of a lack of conception of writing as something that might be a valuable part of a shared intellectual enterprise, productive and useful in its own right. I see it as far too often an activity that is undertaken without any clear rationale other than its part of a set of set of classroom routines. . . . If teachers were engaged in a more productive, meaningful way as writers themselves I think they'd be less likely to encourage/insist on their students producing rather artificial school genres that are not intrinsically meaningful or connected with writing in the real world.

(John Yandell, in interview, Andrews 2008)

It is true that the classroom can present a limited view of what writing can be, its potential for creativity, development of thought and personal growth. Writing is in many ways an unnatural activity. However, it is an activity of great power and one that, when people begin to think about their relationships with it, touches us profoundly. We write for ourselves and we write at significant moments in our lives, so that the words on the screen, but far more often on paper, allow us to reach out to others. Of the language modes it is the one that all of us, even English teachers, are most likely to fear. Even those who publish regularly, who are prizewinning novelists, essayists and poets, even they speak of the daunting nature of the blank page. However, writing also brings happiness. Every writer and teacher of writing brings with them a complex history of their own encounters with writing. An awareness of the mixed feelings that even the youngest child may have about making marks on the page can be helpful to the teacher. It is useful for us to think about our own histories as writers and to consider what we know about writing and how we can use that to review and inform our practice.

It has become a regular activity in new writing groups to reflect on our writing histories. This allows us, individually and collectively, to think about the whole complex business of writing. The outcomes are always interesting and often emotional. It makes us think about the experiences that we are creating for those we teach. What arises, both in the moment a group shares some of their memories, and, later, looking at the patterns of what people say about writing, is a an emerging affective, intellectual and social map of ordinary writing – which is extraordinary. In recalling important moments from our lives as writers, we find ourselves mapping some of the territory.

We often begin with fragments of memory written on sticky notes (see end of chapter). Sharing and discussion of these can lead to a more extended piece of writing. Some groups and all PGCE students with whom we work write a longer history of themselves as writers. This chapter draws on data from these activities. These are memories that come most easily to mind so perhaps significant in shaping our understandings of writing. They are also written with others, so there may be a zeitgeist, or memories prompted by the memories of others. What follows is the beginning of our analysis of these fragments.

Teachers' early memories are those of making a mark: on sand, on the pavement, on walls and floorboards, on desks and cupboard doors to declare a presence, and in places that provoke a reaction – on the pages of a parent's precious book, on the about-to-be wallpapered wall, for posterity, on what was a first father's day card and which he keeps still. First, marks are important and then names; one's own and those of family and friends. Early on, we learn the power of naming; 'Writing my *name* on school books, birthday cards . . .' writes one teacher, and another:

> I always had to write my name on the 1st page of a new book. Loved the freshness of the page and marking my ownership of the book.

The magic of nouns and the way that writing can be a kind of magic is learned early and remains:

> Writing out his name – over and over and over and over . . .

At the same time, technical skills must be mastered and we develop preferences for the materials we use. David Barton (1994) points out the potential difficulty of there being only the one word 'writing' to indicate both composition and transcription. That confusion, and what sometimes seems an overemphasis on the transparency of the technical – and the concomitant difficulty in engaging with composition and style – colours many people's view of writing.

We remember handwriting practice with pleasure and pain. Left-handers often mention pencil grip, smudged letters and extra practice which didn't work. We remember 'writing between the lines', mixing up 'p', 'b' and 'd' and 'having to even out the stick parts'. Some of us were proud of our neat handwriting and remember conscious changes in style:

> Writing joined up! I remember going through TONS of practice in junior school to write the way I do now. [This writer has exceedingly neat and precise handwriting.]

Others remember their hands hurting in exams and their dislike of their handwriting:

> I used to get dad to write the track lists out on my tapes as I didn't like my scruffy writing.

Closely linked to handwriting is the rite of passage that is the pen licence and the imposition of what implements may be used:

> Having to write in a fat red pencil at school always – it being really special when we were allowed to write in Biro occasionally.

> Being told by my geography teacher to write in pencil because I wasn't ready to use pen. (I was in Year 9)

And then there is spelling. Some of us take to it like ducks to water. We remember the 'little green spelling book and the discovery that "this morning" was not "smorning"'.

> First spelling test – and getting full marks ☺ in primary school and then writing stories which included those words.

For others spelling becomes a barrier:

> I found it difficult to write stories because I was always worried about my spelling, how it appeared on the page or whether it was good enough.

> Writing ¾ of a page of A4 and then throwing it away because I had made a spelling error. The rubbish bin overflowing.

> The joy I had in Year 2 when our teacher told us not to worry about spelling but just to 'have a go' writing a story and to let it take us where we wanted. It felt like flying after years of writing being a struggle.

We do need to be able to form letters and use them to spell conventionally. It is good to be able to write legibly and type quickly. The paper and words chosen, the adherence to conventions remain important. 'I always spend an age thinking of how to open texts and e-mails: Hey! Howdy! Good morning! Which is best? ☺' However, most writing memories concern writing that matters to the writer, and to their reader, which is some-times themselves. The most frequent reference is to writing letters and e-mails. Here is writing for a very particular audience, affirming love and connection, understanding the impact of words on the page. Letters are written to friends and distant relatives; on 'blue paper' to fathers, brothers, husbands away on military service; to future partners and to grandparents. Although teachers mention e-mails, letters seem to be mentioned more often. Is it because of their material nature?

> A small note to a friend written on the back of a raffle ticket when he was leaving work – he still has it in his wallet.

Another teacher remembers writing letters to friends after graduation 'and not simply going online and Facebooking them'. Even the back of a raffle ticket has something of the personal about it. Letters are where love can be found: the letter written to a new boyfriend who is now her husband and which 25 years on, he still has; the one 'to be opened by my husband on the morning of our wedding day' and another written to a grandfather, 'thanking him for everything he had done for me. It made him cry'. This writing signals relationship and may prompt a response like the one sent by a grandmother to a granddaughter who had broken up with a boy she loved, 'she underlined the words for emphasis'.

At an NWP workshop this writer remembered writing home from school:

> It was writing letters home from Boarding School. I was sent to a 1950's boarding school in Eldoret, Kenya, 500 miles away from my home in Uganda. I was six and a half years old. Every week we would sit and write a letter home. It had to be in our neatest handwriting, have no mistakes and wasn't supposed to contain any true accounts of beatings, poor food, sickness, etc. It had to be positive. I remember the sacredness of those letters, how they concentrated love into a prayer for my absent mother and father. Writing home was like an act of worship, every little movement of the pen sacred, and every word drenched in home-sick love.
>
> My new writing . . . a teacher insisting on neatness . . . silent, pain-filled devotion, homesickness, aching empathy.
>
> Even as I write this, 54 years later, I feel the tears making my vision blurred, so that every letter I'm writing has a ghost-double on the page.

When the writer shared this he found his experience was echoed by a fellow teacher whose honest letter home had been torn up before her at her boarding school: similar heartbreaks. This writer signals, also, the importance of the safe space. Looking back at the workshop he wrote:

> There's something special about sharing writing in a circle of other writers. Is it shared vulnerability? As writers, we want to express ourselves in this form, but making the work public exposes us to potential criticism from others. However, if everyone round the circle is in the same situation it changes the risk . . .
>
> Whatever, still a bit teary when I volunteered to read out my memories of writing in Africa as a 7 year old, I felt immense support from all those there, as though they understood where I was coming from. Not insignificant was the very sensitive way you both handled the moment. You saw and respected that I was talking about something personally precious.

For some writing comes easy. Others prefer different ways of thinking and self-expression. We need to respect that. However, amongst, now, hundreds of pre-service teachers it is rare to find many who have had not one good experience of writing.

We learn the rituals of writing: the thank you letters at Christmas and birthdays, variously disliked, and the letter to Father Christmas where early powers of persuasion are exercised and later refined when a tooth is swallowed or a cat or dog dearly wanted. These may be precursors to letters of complaint and explanation which some find cathartic. Others talk about writing in diaries where, in the course of writing, anger dissipates or hurt is soothed and where the unsent letter can be found:

> Letters written but not given when my sister was in hospital.

> From seven I wrote a diary and shared with the page all I couldn't share in real life. I could write the unsayable in my diary – yet still self-censored, aware of an imaginary audience. I wonder if writing is simultaneously a shameful activity and liberation from shame. Rereading these diaries, it seems I wrote to my future adult, a forgiving grown up – or, alternatively, to tell this adult 'this is who you are, where you come from.'

Some keep travel journals alongside e-mails sent home; 'trying to capture the essence of each location'. Some mention the deep feelings connected with diary writing: promises to oneself; private writing and the violation when others read it. Writing touches on big life events:

> writing my will – very scary

> words for my father's funeral

> writing and performing a poem for my husband on our wedding day.

> on the back of an envelope about my daughter when she was 16 weeks old. This was an observation of her first four months. This included the weather on the night we brought her home. What we did. Who we saw.

Writing derives from who we are and it can shape us in ways we may not have expected.

> It's 1991 and I am drafting a letter that will go to 4,000 secondary schools announcing a potential SATs boycott. This letter will define me for years to come.

The job application and CV is often mentioned. This is high-stakes writing that may determine what will happen to you next. So much writing that teachers and pre-service teachers mention has a great deal resting on it. No wonder that we feel ambivalent about writing. Whilst one teacher may write:

> As a child I loved being able to sit down in front of a blank piece of paper and invent a story.

many will say:

> assignment writing – the fear of the blank page! It took me ages to realise that just to put down anything really helped.

After letter writing, it is university writing that looms largest. Here, teachers learn to 'write in new ways'. That requirement, 10,000 words, is repeated with incredulity and pride. Writing is an intellectual enterprise and the research, the search for the words – struggling to describe 'sounds' and music. . . . (How can you easily describe the sound of a person's voice?), the 'hammering it out' are aspects of writing that sometimes can be forgotten when teaching. When teachers say they are not writers, they are perhaps thinking of published novelists. One NWP teacher reiterates that she is not a writer but interested in the process 'with a speciality in list-making'. But she writes in detail about her own classroom. This may well be the most powerful thing that a teacher can write, so that her experience and thinking is shared with others.

Writing for and with others plays an important part in teachers' sense of themselves as writers. Many mention writing with cousins, friends and siblings who wrote newspapers, magazines, comics (Lipstick Girl, the superhero) and songs. One writer remembers 'writing fake love letters with a friend on mum's typewriter and posting them to people at school', another wrote a series of 'Fatty Podge' booklets to entertain her brother. Stories and poems are mentioned as frequently as dissertations (stories more frequently than poems) and sometimes these are remembered in connection with praise, a competition won, the work read out or published in some way. More often the writer remembers the content or readers' reactions. Stories about dogs and dinosaurs; adventure stories for a granddad in hospital; stories in the style of Jane Austen and Catherine Cookson; a story with the title 'Along came a spider' and one about Bolton Wanderers' journey through the European Champions League. One teacher simply remembers 'writing lots of stories so I could fill up my writing book and get a new one'.

Quick memories and longer histories remind us of the variety and complexity of being a writer. Writing is not abstract but construed in terms of social practices. It reflects cultural norms and values. Writing may be embedded in family rituals or reflect the demands of certain kinds of education. Writing for and with others is crucial: keeping in touch, going public, marking important life events, friendship, intimacy, endings. It is worth bearing in mind when working with young writers.

Moments from my writing life

We recommend this activity for an early writers' meeting. This is what we do:

- Ask everyone to take four or five sticky notes – they could have more if they wish.
- On each note, they should write one memory of writing: it can be from any time in their lives and about any aspect of writing. There is room only for a headline indication of the memory: *writing to the tooth fairy, writing on the walls of the house; I'm left-handed so I often smudge what I've written, using proper ink pens at school was a nightmare!; writing Catherine Cookson-style stories. . . . inspired by visits to the mobile library.* Invite writers to add the age they were at the time of each memory.
- Arrange the notes in chronological order. Attach them to the walls so that they form an easily read display. If wall space is limited, they can be stuck to strips of till roll and laid out around the room.
- Take time to read and enjoy each other's writing memories.
- Choose one event and write the story of it.

When you have written memories of writing, you may wish to write at greater length about one of the moments you have recalled. Also, look back over your list – and those of others if you are writing in a group – and think about all the many purposes and pleasures of writing, and the objects, people, places and feeling which surround the experience of writing. We have found that when we think about writing in this way, we begin to think about teaching it in a different way.

My writing life

Use these prompts to help you write about your own history as a writer. You do not need to respond to every prompt. Use them as a guide.

- Can you remember learning to write? Do you still have some examples?
- What has been easy and pleasurable? What has been difficult?
- What kind of writing do you remember from your education: schools, colleges, university?
- What kind of writing have you undertaken at home: encouraged/enforced by family?
- When do you write for yourself? Do you write a diary, a journal, letters, e-mail, stories, poetry, articles, essays, manifestos . . .?
- What are the landmark texts in your life?
- Has there been a time in your life when you were compelled to write, or were not able to write?
- Who do you write for?
- Handwriting, spelling, typing, punctuation. Do you love or loathe them?
- What places and equipment do you particularly think of when you think about writing?
- What has been influential in your development as a writer?
- Who or what has helped you to write? Who or what has made it difficult for you to write?
- How has your reading influenced how and what you write?
- Reflect on the ways in which your knowledge and experience of writing has an impact on your teaching and your understanding of what happens in the classroom.

References

Andrews, R, (2008) *The Case for a National Writing Project for Teachers*. Reading: CfBT Education Trust.

Barton, D. (1994) *Literacy: An Introduction to the Ecology of Written Language*. Oxford: Blackwell Publishers.

Chapter 6

Setting up a teachers' writing group

In a teachers' writing group, thinking about writing and about teaching writing go hand in hand. In the first instance, it is an opportunity for teachers to have a practice of writing in the same way that music or art teachers engage in those arts for their own sake. Consideration of teachers' writing in a mutually supportive group informs the development of their practice as teachers.

Number of participants

The ideal number for a group will depend on where you are able to meet and how formal your group is. If the group is a voluntary arrangement, attendance is likely to fluctuate according to health, school meetings, examination pressures and so on. Something between twelve and twenty-four is a good number. Those who meet in public spaces depend on where they can sit together which, in a gallery or other public space is usually the café. Too large a group in such a space can feel intrusive and it becomes more difficult to speak to the group as a whole. However, whatever the size of the group that arrives (we have known a group of two sometimes and as many as twenty-two), if it is not a formal course or project, welcome, and tolerate, a much larger constituency than actually arrives for every meeting. The existence of a group that meets regularly and which keeps all those interested informed, means that there is always somewhere for teachers to come to write and to share their thinking with sympathetic others. Everyone may see the website and have access to what their group is doing. When a group starts, some meetings may attract only a few people. Keep going. Once established, a session might attract as many as thirty-five. Welcome teachers from all phases. The mixture of experience enriches the whole.

Where to meet

Ideally, groups should be able to meet in a fixed meeting room. A school or university can provide the kind of space that works well with access to facilities for refreshments. Groups who begin by meeting in a public venue often find that they wish to find a more permanent meeting space, so that it is easier to discuss each other's writing and teaching. Some groups have found a public room; one over a pub, or at an existing writer's centre. There is some virtue in meeting in people's homes, but as a general rule this is not such a good idea if the group is to be inclusive.

How often

Most groups meet at least twice a term. Some groups meet less frequently. Where it is possible to meet more often, once or twice a month, say, a group can gain momentum and build some aspect of practice. We know that it is often difficult for teachers to meet as often as they would like.

How to communicate

Someone in the group needs to have a database of contact details of all participants. E-mail is the most common way of communicating information. Some groups use social media and all groups may have access to a secure group section of the NWP UK website. Reminders about the date and location of meetings are important. Don't be discouraged by uneven attendance!

Getting started: key elements and possible structures

The structure of a meeting will depend on the preferences of the group. Two or three hours is a good length of time, depending on the time of day. Some groups like to start with a drink, or have a coffee break halfway through. Those times when individuals and groups can get together and talk are a crucial part of our development. Good biscuits or homemade cake are an added bonus! We may joke about cake and biscuits, but the atmosphere of the group is important. The care taken in providing a comfortable and congenial space signals the value placed upon each individual and the work that they are doing.

All meetings should include time for teachers to write for themselves. Beware! Even if they have come to write, teachers are likely to resist. A key strategy for avoidance is to talk. Talk is welcome, but there comes a point where writing must happen and a group leader must gently insist on it. A good strategy is to ask for a short burst of writing in the first instance. Explain it is not to be shared. It can just be something like: how did I get here? Teachers should write for themselves as individuals, not as teachers and not in role as children. It may well be that the ideas for writing that are proposed can be adapted for the classroom, but, in the first instance, teachers write for their own purposes and pleasure. It is through that experience that teachers who attend the meetings are able to think and rethink their own writing practice and pedagogy. Most meetings should include time for teachers to share what they have written and to respond to each other's writing. All meetings should include time to focus on the teaching of writing.

The shape of the meeting is likely to depend on the group leader. We will suggest one possible pattern that is tried and tested. You would be able to adapt this to suit the needs of a group. Before anything, however, we recommend that all participants have a **writing notebook or journal** (Chapter 7). Where we have secured funding (and often when we have not) we have supplied teachers with a notebook at their initial meeting. The provision of notebooks for writing conveys a strong message about the value of writing and the worth of the individual as a writer. The subsequent introduction of journals to a classroom, accompanied by the freedom to write personally and in ways that are important to the individual, can be the single most influential step that teachers make when they first join a writing group. Writing teachers soon find their own preferred writing materials and bring these with them. But have paper ready, sometimes teachers arriving hotfoot from an after-school meeting have not had time to pick up their own. After an initial welcome, and introductions where necessary, a meeting might follow this pattern:

- A writing **warm up** which might begin with single **words** or very short piece of writing that could be shared immediately. You might start or follow on with some **freewriting** that may or may not be shared.
- One or two pieces of more **sustained writing** that form the main focus of that session. How these are structured will depend on the nature of the writing. It may be that there is a preparatory short piece followed by time for more sustained writing. However, the pattern of writing may well vary from week to week. Once a group is established it is a good idea to make time for people to start at least one longer piece of writing. There are ideas throughout this book which may prompt more sustained writing projects. This will be ideal for some teachers. Others like the immediate prompt and opportunity to write offered by the workshop alone. Once groups are established people may decide to include the time to write pieces of their own choice. However a writing exercise might begin, expect, encourage even, everyone to use the initial idea in a way that suits them. There is no need to slavishly follow the introductory prompts unless there is a very clear reason for doing so. What happens when we hear how individuals have worked with an initial idea often helps us to see the idea more flexibly and to see, also, how we might use that idea within our teaching.

Quite recently we used a poem by Robert Crawford, *Clan Donald's Call to Battle At Harlaw*, which we found on the Scottish Poetry Library's website. It is a real rallying cry, an exhortation. It works with short lines, going through the alphabet, mostly two lines to a letter and using the imperative construction: 'be . . .' We noticed that there are a mixture of nouns and adjectives, 'be eagles, be elegant'; it is both serious and funny, 'Be knightly, be niftiest'; there are Scots words and sometimes a surprise – 'be off now/be up for it'. So, there is a pattern and it is an exhortation. We talked a little about possibilities: facing Year 9 on a Friday afternoon; the supermarket shop; cooking the Sunday roast. What was prompted by a battle cry became: advice about how to get on the 5:45 train to Sheringham; a rallying cry for Spring to arrive; an address to small sons at bath time, subverting the structure and patterning the writing with: 'this is your first warning', 'this is your second warning'; an address to four-year-old superheroes, conjuring that early years play space and written in words they could enjoy; a magnificent prelude to performance for a barbershop choir and lines full of hope written for the writer's children. Rather cheesy, she said, before she began. Not cheesy at all, we said.

I started writing this poem at Writing Teachers, and finished it later at home. I enjoyed having the tight structure of the poem to work from. My children are 4 and 7 years old, and I wanted to write the poem for them. My daughter helped with some of the words and the title. She is really excited to have a poem written for her and wants to stick it on her wall. I have also used this poem as a starting point for some writing with my Creative Writing Group (Years 7 and 8) and they also enjoyed writing their own rallying cries for various audiences.

Be YOU!
(To my children)
Be adventurous
Be brave and busy
Be caring, curious, calm and crazy
Be different
Be enthusiastic, explorative and empathetic
Be fearless, be full of fun, be a friend
Be giving and generous
Be happy, honest and hopeful
Be intense, interested and imaginative
Be joyful
Be kind
Be loyal and loving, be a listener
Be magical and magnificent
Be nice to yourself
Be open minded, be original
Be playful, perceptive and passionate
Be quiet sometimes, be questioning, be quirky
Be real, be resilient, be reflective
Be sensitive, be soft-hearted
Be thoughtful and true
Be understanding, be unique
Be vivid, be valiant and venturesome
Be wild and wholehearted
Be yourself
Be you

- Time for **reading and responding** is essential. Here one's idea of what is possible is expanded and a sense of oneself as a writer grows (see Chapter 8).
- A **break** where we find that there is time to **network** and cement friendships.

- **A focus on classroom practice** – this may arise from the writing exercises. Sometimes members of the group will have requested a focus – writing poetry or non-fiction, perhaps, or using the outdoors. Teachers can bring in evidence of something they have done in their own teaching and share it. A powerful activity, especially when you have a group that spans a wide age range, is to have everyone bring in a piece of child's writing. The discussion that arises from looking closely at the range of writing from nursery to A level has made us reassess our understandings of how writing develops, what it is, and how children, and adults, become confident and more accomplished writers.
- Where a group is preparing to write an article or paper, or to contribute to Continuing Professional Development (CPD), the balance of the session might change. There will always be time for personal writing, but this may be curtailed so that there is time for discussion and preparation of ideas and materials. Equally, on some occasions, the writing takes longer or allows for discussion of pedagogy to be woven through writing and responding, so the formal focus on teaching may be diffused.
- There is a value, once a group has become established, in having a **shared project**. It can sharpen the focus of the group's thinking and it paves the way for useful dissemination of what the group is learning. Some groups choose to interview children or track individuals. Sometimes a group might stay with a topic for reflection and research over a period of time. Not only does the person running the session bear this in mind when preparing the activities, but teachers bring related evidence from their classrooms.

Leaders and co-operatives: becoming a facilitator

It is practical to have one or two people who take responsibility for the running of the group. However, it is important that a group is run in a way that honours the principles of professional autonomy and partnership. Responsibilities can be shared and everyone can have the opportunity to lead all or part of a session. There are practical considerations: someone must organise the pattern of meetings and find and book rooms; tea and coffee, if possible; participants need reminders of meetings; and the meeting needs choreographing. To begin with it may be helpful to have one or possibly two people who will do this. The most obvious thing to think about is the pattern of the session. What happens during the meeting is likely to change over time. We have found all the following elements helpful at different times and they are considered in other sections of the book:

- **Journals and writers' notebooks**
- Warm up
- **Freewriting**
- Quick writes
- **Writing metaphors**
- **Writing histories**
- **Reflecting on writing**

- Longer writing
- Collaborative writing
- **Reading and feeding back**
- **Responding face-to-face/online/in writing**

Workshop leaders, and teachers, are always looking for good ideas to prompt and shape writing and writing development. This book includes many such ideas. Chapter 20 lists other sources. The NWP UK website holds popular resources. Try to avoid websites that offer '100 starters for writing' which, while they may, indeed, help you think of an idea, do little more than suggest a title. Try and shape the session so that writing exercises support each other. Think about what processes of thought and of writing may be supported by the activities. Think about how an activity can help the writer think 'slant'; how the resources you use and the approach you offer, help the writer to write in particular ways.

A workshop leader must think about writing prompts, ways of responding, and how the group will engage with classroom practice. However, there is another responsibility which is harder to articulate, and that is the reassurance, nurturing and challenge to writing teachers who may feel unsure of themselves as writers or as teachers of writing.

A facilitator has to think about the people in the group. Writing is something which can make people feel uneasy. Those words on the page may expose something. Better not to write at all. And if they have written, better not to read out. Better to say you have come for ideas for the children. Better to talk about it. Better not to write. Potentially, better not to come at all. We know that many people do feel it is worthwhile to come to the group, even in the dark through country lanes, even after a gruelling day at school, even after waiting twenty minutes for a bus. Because the act of writing, the reading and hearing of writing, the affirmation of fellow writing teachers leaves us lighter, happier somehow. Simply writing together is potent. However, it can become something more with a little thought. There is something to be done that is about affirmation and appreciation. People arrive from the midst of teaching. Their heads are full of other worries and, especially at first, writing themselves can be just another of those worries.

We have found that, even when teachers have signed up for a writing group, many will be nervous and some are surprised, even, that they might be expected to do any writing themselves. Take that into account and think about swimming. Make the pool feel safe for them. Introduce games. Don't insist on the completing of lengths. Be pleased when that happens. Laugh. And come at it slant. Read what writers have to say. Find ways of bringing their ideas to the table.

Being aware of the mood and needs of the group as a whole and of individuals in particular can make a difference to how people feel about writing and reading together. It is not a competition. Think about the space. Can everyone be comfortable? Is it possible for everyone to sit round one table? Is it possible to move people around so they get to know each other? Does everyone know each other's name and teaching context? Are you learning about the members of the group so that you can plan with them in mind?

This year what I have learned about teaching writing . . .

The prompts are important but allow people the space and time to follow their own path. Trust in the group. Allow for gaps and silence and the pause for thought. I do not need to entertain or enthuse or engage, I need to create the opportunity, the intention, the expectation that as writers we are here to write. Sometimes happy to share, Sometimes not. Sometimes a seed is planted that will not grow for a while. And an idea is formed that will come into its own at a later date. A piece of free writing can become the basis of a poem – a list of words the beginning of a story – a childhood memory the skeleton of a memoir. In a writing group the silence is as important as the sharing and the sharing is more important than showing off.

(Teacher educator, primary)

be open; listen; notice; enjoy; affirm; acknowledge complexity; value individuality; value writing; be patient; prompt rather than insist; allow yourself to insist sometimes; vary the context; allow space for responding; read; learn from others; expect surprise

---

Words

Paying attention to the words we choose is crucial; choosing the apt word or phrase, a pleasurable activity.

sludge   Westminster   hugger mugger   flop   feverfew   denizen

We love to begin a workshop with lists of words. This is how it works: make a list of words, five or six, that simply come to mind. They may be words that sound good, have good associations or are simply rattling around in your head. Try not to censor yourself, and try not to show off. Nouns and verbs are good, and short words: try 'and', 'under', 'if'. . . . Proper nouns work well – place names, personal names, brand names, nicknames, slang, dialect words and words in other languages are all good. When everyone has some words written down, read aloud. Each person says one word from their list. Speak clearly and slowly and leave a short pause after each word spoken. Go around the group three or four times and notice the patterns and surprises, words that made you laugh, the ripple of sound, unexpected juxtapositions.

That's it. Words on the air. It is a bit like an orchestra tuning up. Get words out there. We are reminded of words, introduced to words, find them as unlikely neighbours:

barnacle, plug, conspire, ball bearing, girder, although, Constantinople, sandwich, calamity, cheesy, nincompoop . . .

Sometimes people feel that they have 'done that activity' and don't repeat it, but we find that it is different every time. We have also noted that it encourages young writers, especially, to seek out interesting words. As they get used to the activity, so their choice of words become more interesting. They (and we) realise the power of a proper noun or of a word like 'if'. We stop having to say 'mellifluous' and find a more interesting way of saying 'chocolate'. We notice, also, how words work together; we notice alliteration; unexpected pairings; accidental sequences; blunt words mocking grand ones; themes developing.

Variations

- Ask for specific words that may anticipate the writing that follows – the names of sweets, parts of a machine, the verbs of tools and gadgets, things you might find in a handbag or pocket. Such lists often lead into another piece of writing.
- Ask for specific parts of speech: prepositions, verbs (insist on finite forms), proper nouns. These may well anticipate a particular genre.
- What 'stories' or anecdotes are provoked by these words? In what contexts might any of these words carry weight or be forbidden?
- Look for words and phrases that you like in newspapers or books. Introduce texts containing specialist vocabulary and have writers choose from them: cycle maintenance; insect identification; street guides; paint charts; maps.
- Encourage writers to note down words they hear and like to add to their own lists.

Following on

- Follow the list making with **freewriting**. Challenge writers to include as many of their words as they can into the writing.
- Look at your list of words and note the connections; circle the word you like most and use it to prompt a piece of writing; circle and join a pattern of words to shape a piece of writing.
- Invite writers to use, judiciously, some others' words in a new piece of their own writing – or use a word's association to spark off a 'riff' of writing.
- A list of words with a theme or names of sweets, for example, provide a starting point for writing. The list making activates the memory. The words around the group prompt further ideas 'ooh, yes, sherbet dib dabs'. The space between the original making of the list, through the sharing of words and then anecdotes, quickly generates material for writing.

- When working with children, ask them to tell you why they chose certain words. Often the single word will carry the weight of a story with it: from the word, to the telling, to the writing!
- Some texts yield technical terms that can be shaped into found poems – the Yellow Pages, car manuals, atlases, recipe books. Look up *Silent Poem* by Robert Francis, which consists of four columns of compound nouns. Lists of words arranged rhythmically and with attention to sound can create great performance poems.

Chapter 7

Notebooks

notebook; journal; day book; writer's notebook; log; think book; blog; diary; sketchbook

write often; write a lot; draw; make diagrams; write as you want to write; note down what your eyes see, your ears hear, your heart feels; fill up the pages; always remember to note down the date and time; write freely; enjoy your journal; read it back to yourself; add more and more; make it your own; make it unique, just as you are unique

> A journal can be entirely private, but it becomes much more powerful if you can use it to open up conversations with at least one other.
>
> (Toby Fulwiler, NATE Conference, York, 1988)

The journal or notebook is essential for the writer. It is where the writing teacher's journey often becomes a reality and the entry point for a change of teaching style in their classrooms. A notebook is where writing happens, and what that looks like is entirely up to the writer – the owner of that notebook. You may write with other materials and for different reasons, but the notebook is yours. It is not to be marked or assessed. You may choose the kind of notebook and writing implement that you prefer and you may write just as you wish. The notebook signals freedom: the freedom to try things out; to write clumsy or ridiculous sentences; to be self-indulgent, unreasonable, outrageous; to forget punctuation and to make up words. Your notebook allows you to cover the ground – lots of words and perhaps not so much sense; it allows you to experiment; you can take risks, including the risk of writing badly; you can gather up carefully crafted fragments. How you use the notebook and what you call it may change at different times in your writing life. You may have more than one notebook at a time, each with a different purpose. You may choose to gather everything in one place.

In his preface to *Writers and their Notebooks* (Raab 2010), Philip Lopate describes writing as 'one way of self-making' and celebrates the metaphors which the essayists in this book use to describe their notebooks:

> a laboratory, a mirror, a brainstorming tool, an icebreaker, a wailing wall,
>   a junk drawer, a confessional, a postcard to oneself, singing in the shower,

a playground for the mind, . . . an observation sharpener, a survival kit, . . .
a witness stand, a therapist, a housekeeper, a spiritual advisor, a compost bin,
a punching bag, a sounding-board, a friend.

(p. vii)

It is where you – and children who have journals – can develop your writing voice
and where you can flex your muscles in many different ways. It is simply true that if
you write every day, even for ten minutes only, your writing and how you feel about it
changes in positive ways.

The notebook is an important element of the writing group. This personal space for
writing plays its part in a teacher becoming a teacher who writes. It signals the value of
writing and of the person who writes. It is where you will collect ideas, write for yourself, write with a group. It is where you will write whenever, wherever, whatever you
wish. We all, adults and children, will become better writers by writing, for ourselves,
about things that matter to us. The notebook allows you to place, within firm covers,
writing that is, initially at least, for yourself alone. Writing teachers use the notebook
in as many ways as there are writing teachers. Some like an elaborate notebook which
they decorate with images and pockets for lists of words and found texts; some prefer
a more understated notebook, plain or lined, which does not impose high expectations
upon the writer, but is happy to embrace notes, scribbles, train tickets, pen or pencil.
Some save their notebook solely for the writing workshops so they have a record not
only of their own writing, but also the ideas that have prompted the writing. There is
a continuum, also, of the intimately personal to much more public writing which is in
preparation for sharing of some kind.

The notebook – and other stationery

As we have said, the notebook should fit your needs and preferences. Some people have
two or three notebooks for different places – one small enough to slip into a pocket or
bag, an A5 notebook that is easily carried around, an A4 notebook to be kept in one
place, at home or in the workplace. Plain or lined paper is a matter of personal prefer-
ence, soft- or hard-backed, spiral or sewn binding. A spiral-bound notebook is easier to
manipulate when a table is not available, but it is also easier to rip out the pages. The
computer and the easily torn page can remove the mistakes and mistaken judgements
which are often worth keeping. Be brave enough to keep the mess. Toby Fulwiler
(1987) in *The Journal Book* recommends a loose-leaf notebook so that you can rear-
range writing into different sections but others suggest that you should choose a bound
book so that it is hard to tear out the pages. Certainly, re-reading past entries, even
those which you wanted to dispose of, can be interesting and useful. Each of us will find
the stationery that works for us. Many of us will be glad of the excuse to browse the
shelves for 'the one'!

Ideally, you should always carry your notebook. You never know when there might
be something that you wish to write down, or a spare few minutes to write. In *The*

Thirteen Secrets of Poetry, Adrian Mitchell advises children to take a notebook with them everywhere. One mixed Year 3/4 class were given little origami books to carry with them and could be seen at lunchtime capturing fish and chips, dinner ladies' sayings and terrible jokes. In another school a group of boys are writing spies, out at break time jotting down what is, and may be, going on. Increasingly, the computer or iPad holds the writer's notebook. Beware its capacity to remove chunks of text. Rejoice in the possibilities of including images of all kinds and links to other texts.

When shall I write?

Often. Write as often as you can, at least two or three times a week, ideally every day. It can be helpful to write at the same time every day, but don't be so fixated on doing so that a failure to keep to time results in completely giving up. Write early in the morning, late at night, on the bus to work, at 3pm with a cup of tea. Write when you notice something, want to remember something, want to practice or try something out. Write when you have a problem to solve, a decision to make, confusions to untangle. Ann Berthoff claims that 'anybody concerned with working out ideas could, should, must be – willy-nilly – a writer, because writing provides the readiest means of carrying out what I. A. Richards calls an *audit of* meaning. Writing as a way of knowing. It is where writing happens' (in Raab 2010). Write for the sheer pleasure of it, as a work out, a dance of words, a meditation.

Where shall I write?

Anywhere. Some people do like to write regularly in the same place and set up that space comfortably for writing. Others talk about writing in cafés or on train journeys. Mothers speak of writing at the kitchen table. Writing teachers write with their regular writing group and with their pupils. There are no rules.

How should I write?

Freely. As we have said before, you should write in whatever way you wish. Do not worry about formal writing conventions. Break rules. Take risks. Develop your voice. Write long entries as often as possible to help develop ideas fully. Write lists. Make lots of entries. Quantity is a measure of a good journal. So don't worry about whatever it is that you think is rubbish. Note the date (and time) of each entry. Whilst it is obvious what date it is when you are writing, when you read back it can be infuriating not to know.

What should I write?

Whatever you wish. These notebooks are places where teachers, and students, become writers. The more you write the better, and the greater your sense of ownership the better. Writer's notebooks can be the focal point for all kinds of recording, imagining and generating of ideas. Many writers, writing about writing, talk about the need to get the words on the page, and those who write about writing notebooks value quantity. They recognise that much of what they write may not be useful or even of any quality but they see themselves as getting words on the page. We see it as the equivalent of distance running for an athlete. It builds stamina. It helps you to know your body and its limits and horizons, or in this case, the limits and horizons of the writing self.

The notebook is a place to collect ideas and to experiment. Some writers draw as well as write. Notebooks are a good place to store photos, found text, snippets from newspaper, jokes, in fact anything that you might want to use in your writing. Include a place for words you love. Listen to words spoken around you. Write down words from menus, signs, books, newspapers, essays, e-mails, maps . . . A writer's notebook might have a more purposeful connection to a crafted piece of writing, although the line between that and a journal is a fine one. In some contexts it may usefully signal a more public status. Andrew Cowan (2011) in *The Art of Writing Fiction* recommends that the fiction writer should keep several different notebooks for different purposes: a weather notebook, one for work, one for daily domestic events . . .

Often, when adults begin writing for themselves, they find themselves turning to autobiography and self-reflection. Many find that they are writing about deeply personal things and that the writing is helpful and important to them. There is never any compulsion to share writing from a journal, though often writers in a group do share with at least one other reader. Some writers like to use writing to develop their thinking. In the 1980s, Pat D'Arcy (1989) and teachers in Wiltshire had great success with what they called 'think books'. Children used their notebooks to ask questions and to develop ideas, others used them to collect scientific observations and to develop understandings of the natural world. Notebook writing does not inevitably lead to fiction or poetry. It may be that you like to write about experiences and ideas that lead to exposition and argument. We have used notebooks extensively to capture the life of classrooms and then to reflect on what we have seen. There is more about using reflective teaching journals in Chapter 13.

It is not always easy to decide what to write. The blank pages remain daunting even for those of us who have been using notebooks for years. Books listed in Chapter 20 suggest ideas for adult writers. *Children's Writing Journals* (Graham & Johnson 2003) is a helpful starting point for primary schools. In the early stages of any teacher's involvement with writing groups, freewriting and the use of journals becomes a significant part of their changed practice. Here are two accounts, one from a secondary teacher and the other from a primary school teacher, on the impact of using journals in school:

> So many of the comments that students make about creative writing journals are so positive, moving even. They write about the freedom that a creative writing journal affords them, "Having a private writing journal gives me freedom to write without boundaries" (KS3 student); they write about a sense of honesty and empowerment in their writing that a right to privacy can enable, "I feel honest and every word

I write is true" (KS3); many students are so keen to explore the potential of writing that excites them because it has a genuine sense of their own voice, "You can write it in your journal so that you know you have a copy of your really good idea, and if it feels embarrassing in the moment, you can take the best bit and re-write it before you share." (KS3) It is clear to me that this is a writing experience that goes far beyond the classroom; it does have the potential to be a writing experience that leads to learning about self. From a teaching point of view, creative writing journals have proven to be an invaluable motivator, from a personal point of view, my own creative journal is both resource and respite to cherish.

Some of the evidence, however, would suggest that the process of freewriting and the privacy of a writing journal does not suit everybody. "I have a journal purely because I don't want anyone to read it, including myself." (Year 8 student) She went on to write that "freewriting is silly and I never know what to put." Evidently, where some students relish the freedom that journal writing affords, others are daunted or perhaps sceptical about its usefulness. Emotional readiness is, perhaps, an essential factor in the potential to enjoy and therefore benefit from the practice of journal based freewriting. Emotional readiness will also inform the willingness to share snippets of writing and absorb and reflect verbal feedback, an essential part of the process of developing powerful writing skills. Creative writing demands a personal response, sometimes an emotional response, as well as an intellectual one. Based on my own experience of journal freewriting, and of sharing writing within a group where I felt sharing was safe and welcome, I believe that emotional resilience and confidence can grow as a result of these forms of writing.

(Secondary teacher)

I have given all the children in my class (Year 5) their own writing journals. They can use these for their own writing and write about whatever they want – poems, fiction, stories etc. They can keep them and use them at home or at school. I have also set aside free writing slots where I write in my own writing journal with the children. I couldn't believe how enthusiastic they were over the idea of having their own journals where they can write about whatever they choose. They also found it exciting that I was writing with them. They all wanted to read what I had written and they were also very interested in what my writing looked like. One girl asked me if she could cross things out in her writing. When I showed her my writing, and all my editing and crossing out and scribbling, she found it fascinating. I think the children get lectured about presentation so much, they feel they can't edit their work, as they don't want it to look messy. Hopefully, by seeing my work, they will realise I'm more interested in what they have written, than in what it looks like.

(Primary teacher)

A notebook is a conversation with yourself. It is your job as a writer to keep up the conversation.

Sometimes it is useful to have something to start with. Here are some suggestions, in no particular order:

- Lists: we love lists because they are such a good way of breaking into the blank page, for prompting memory and, sometimes, for finding unexpected connections. The simplest lists might be of words: a list of all the chairs you can think of might prompt a longer piece of writing. Another kind of list is one that acts as a kind of memoir: all the houses you have ever lived in, the cars you have owned, coats that you have worn (coats are a good starter, and so are shoes). See 'Hey Remember That Time . . .' in Chapter 12.

- The stories we tell: Metzger (1992) suggests we list these and provides 'a list of lists'. The lists themselves can become a poem or give rise to longer pieces of autobiographical writing. Her lists include: stories from your childhood; stories your family tell about their lives – and about you; stories that are traditionally repeated at family events; stories that you tell about yourself when you meet someone new; lies you have told so often they have become true . . .

- Word banks, word hoards: collect the words from workshops; note words and phrases as you go about your day – found texts, delicious sounding words, unusual words, solid Anglo-Saxon words, technical words; take a handful to get started or to use as a challenge.

- What I love. Think about something (not a person) that means a great deal to you and with which you have a long experience. Describe it so that you capture what is special about it. People have written about walking the dog, their garden pond, a fountain pen, cycling, a birch tree, sitting down for coffee and the papers on a Sunday morning.

- Write letters, that you don't or can't send: to say something important; to someone who has left or who is no longer alive; to the tooth fairy or Dracula or Superman; to family members, near and far. Letters are a very good form to choose when helping writers to realise their own voices.

- Use a postcard to start a poem or story: you can begin just by describing what you can see.

- Sentence starters are great prompts: I dream of . . .; Once . . .; Sometimes I wonder . . .; On the way to . . .; I wish . . .; Investigate Kenneth Koch, *Wishes, Lies and Dreams* (1970).

- Whatever the reason for your writing, non-stop writing is worthwhile. Peter Elbow (1981) suggests ways of working with the words that appear when you write freely, removing the editor in your head.

References

Cowan, A. (2011) *The Art of Writing Fiction*. Harlow: Pearson Education.

D'Arcy, P. (1989) *Making Sense, Shaping Meaning: Writing in the Context of a Capacity-based Approach to Learning*. Ports, NH: Boynton/Cook.

Elbow, P. (1981) *Writing with Power: Techniques for Mastering the Writing Process*. New York, Oxford: Oxford University Press.

Fulwiler, T. (1987) Workshop handout. NATE conference, York.

Graham, L. & Johnson, A. (2003) *Children's Writing Journals*. Royston: UKLA.

Koch, K. (1970) *Wishes, Lies, and Dreams: Teaching Children to Write Poetry*. New York: Harper & Row.

Metzger, D. (1992) *Writing for your Life*. New York: HarperSanFrancisco A Division of Harper Collins.

Raab, D. M. (2010) *Writers and their Notebooks*. Columbia, South Carolina: University of South Carolina Press.

Chapter 8

Responding

> The one time writing was shared was *excruciating*. New to secondary school, the teacher told me to read my work aloud. I read with head bowed, blushing furiously and she berated me for reading badly. I was pleased with the writing and wouldn't have minded sharing . . . but ALOUD? This was unexpected, disastrous. I *hated* her! Since then, I've never forced anyone to share their writing. But it seems now, to teacher me, that refusal to share is selfish, shows unhealthy self-consciousness. In my dream classroom, students share willingly, expressively, confidently. So why have I never created this atmosphere? I must have partly backed off because of my own memories. Sometimes in class, friends will cajole each other to read aloud and they'll do so with a kind of resigned, yet delighted, air. Exposure, which is inevitable when all writing is autobiographical, seems equally desired and feared.
>
> (Secondary teacher)

> Not many people [in general] are willing or able to give the kind of feedback which helps. People, mostly, don't mind reading what I've written if I ask them, but they rarely want to say anything about it. This is the power of a writing group, the supportive reading and responding. It's probably the idea that has had the greatest impact on my teaching of writing.
>
> (Secondary teacher)

Sharing writing and responding to the writing of others lies at the heart of the writing group. It is the time when writing teachers learn about writing, about themselves as writers, about their own writing and how they wish to write. It is where they experience reading their own work aloud and develop an understanding of how conferencing can work for them as a writer. They learn how this will be at the centre of their own teaching; the taproot for the growing writer. One of the most significant things that a writer learns is to be a reader of their own work. Donald Murray (1982) describes this as 'the other self'.

> The act of writing might be described as a conversation between two workmen muttering to each other at the work bench. The self speaks, the other self listens and responds. The self proposes, the other self considers. The self makes, the other

self evaluates. The two selves collaborate: a problem is spotted, discussed, defined; solutions are proposed, rejected, suggested, attempted, tested, discarded, accepted.

(Murray 1982: 165)

He suggests that the self writes and the other self reads. This is not the reading of a completed text, but a 'sophisticated reading that monitors writing before it is made, as it is made and after it is made' (Murray 1982). It is the other self that might be that disapproving editor in the head that tells us everything is wrong and asks where the interesting connectives are. Our other self may need re-educating, or be discovered under the rubble of maxims and mnemonics from our schooling. The *Transforming Writing* project has coined the phrase 'meta-cognitive manager' to describe something similar to the other self (Rooke 2012). The structures teachers have developed for formative assessment, which is a way of describing the work of the conference, are worth considering. However, the project's conceptualisation of the process of writing and of 'good writing', requires careful scrutiny. What might the meta-cognitive manager be saying to young writers who afford him lodgings? Herein lies the strength of a writing group. When the time comes to share what she has written, the writing teacher learns to know her other self and gains a greater understanding of what needs to be known when teaching. Allow the time, always, for the teacher's experience to be thoroughly her own. Only then will she begin to see how she will enact that experience in her classroom.

A group leader bears in mind the vulnerability of those who write. Years of hearing how bad one's writing is, how crooked the handwriting, how poor the spelling, how feeble the choice of word, how inadequate the thought expressed makes us afraid. Even in a friendly environment it is not easy. Most primary teachers are not English graduates and many secondary teachers, who are, are inhibited by their notion of great writers.

> I am still very nervous about sharing my writing as I feel like everyone else is more 'trained' than myself. I only studied English to GCSE level and feel that all of my experience in English since then (at uni) has been to do with the 'basics' and not extending my experience of creative writing in any way. I feel like everyone else has a better grasp of language and the different structures for writing poetry and that I am still floundering at a very basic level of writing.
>
> (Primary teacher)

> I do not think it takes guts to write, but it sure does take guts to share it.
>
> (Secondary teacher)

Write first. Sharing can come next. It takes courage for many teachers to read aloud and the group leader needs to develop a sensitivity to the group – when to share with the whole group, when to ask for just a sentence or two, when to read in pairs or small groups. Sometimes the time is not right for reading. That is OK. Encourage writers to experience the power of simply sharing a piece of text. One way of getting used to sharing is just to be silly. Short, frivolous writing tasks, written alone or collaboratively, break the ice. Self-consciousness is often drowned in laughter.

In reading aloud, in responding and in hearing others respond we build the shared knowledge that is at the core of a community of writing teachers. We have learned that we are not teaching the writing, but the writer. And in order to do so, first the writer must write for themselves so that we can see what is important to them and where they are. 'I do not know what my students will be able to do until they write without any instructions from me' (Murray 1982).

Then we ask about process. 'Developing writers', as Richard Andrews would have it (Andrews & Smith 2011). Murray (1982) describes how he learned that he was 'teaching what [students] have just learned'. He asks about process and intention or notices what a writer has done, and is able to draw their attention to it so that they develop that meta-cognitive awareness. Georgia Heard (1989), in her excellent chapter about conferring, 'Someone who will truly listen', describes how she moved from a focus on the written product to a focus on the writer.

> I started to teach the writer of the poems, not the poems themselves. . . . When I was a researcher, each poem was valuable to me, no matter how small or unsuccessful. . . . But only if I looked and listened hard enough, trying to hold my evaluations and judgements, could I gather an entire history of each poet. From what they said about their poems I started to understand so much more about them as writers;
>
> (Heard 1989: 39)

You will have noticed, already, how important it is to listen.

> And then finally the teacher as listener. We must be careful not to sacrifice to our roles as error spotters and improvers and correctors that of teacher as listener and reader. I could sum it all up very simply. What is important is that children in school should write about what matters to them to someone who matters to them.
>
> (James Britton, in Pradl 1982)

Appreciative attentive listening

What are we listening to? What are we listening out for? We can learn this first with other writing teachers and then in our classrooms. Since this is a book about teachers' writing groups, we will focus on response in the adult group. Sharing our writing must begin gently. What one sees is how the writer becomes increasingly able to take responsibility for the development of their own writing as a result of sharing and the response of others. It is a movement from safety to risk-taking; from affirmation to the drive to revision. The emphasis on the writer, their intentions and process creates the opportunity for us to think about how to write and how to solve the problems posed for us by the writing. Peter Elbow, whose work on response is the most helpful we know, encourages feedback that reflects the reader's experience back to the writer. In neither approach is it suggested that readers should give direct advice about how to change the text. We must think about how to frame responses which allow the writer to learn about what they have written from others' points of view and how to set about writing what they wish to write. One thing that is very clear from writing groups is that regular, honest and trusted responses over time allow writers to develop beyond expectation. An important question to explore further, is what that trusted response looks like in schools and how it can best be managed.

Ferguson McKay (1987), researching teacher conferences in an undergraduate writing course, used three broad concepts to help him analyse what was happening and to consider why students were making less progress than he hoped. 1. *Confidence and self-image:* did students think of themselves as people who can and do write? 2. *Authority and control:* could students see themselves as authors in command of their writing? 3. *Use of audience responses:* how and when were students able to make use of or reject responses of varied quality? He began to explore these questions using the distinction between *direct instruction* and *encouragement* and came to believe that teacher responses fall at different times along a spectrum between the two. It may be that his early list of distinctions between them could be helpful to us in thinking about response. In Chapter 16 we discuss Peter Elbow's 'Map of Writing' (2000) which charts the range of feedback that a learning writer should expect, moving between privacy and sociability, safety and risk, affirmation and challenge.

Direct instruction	**Encouragement**
Explaining	Listening
Modelling (implicit or explicit)	Receiving, affirming
Persuading	Supporting, confirming
Evaluating	Suggesting changes (I think this goes
Being an authority	in direct instruction)
Correcting	Expressing enthusiasm (sincere)
Often written – indirect	Responding
Manipulation – intentional or	An equal or partner
unintentional	Overlooking some problems
Attention to the written product	Conversational – direct
Criticising	Avoiding manipulation (e.g.
Extensive, detailed comments	manipulative praising)
Definitive interpretation	Attention to the student
	Clarifying
	Few, broad comments
	Speculative and tentative

I have much more confidence in what I write. I know when it sounds good and when it says what I mean.

(Secondary teacher)

Reading aloud

Elbow and Belanoff (1989) suggest that the simple reading aloud of one's writing to one other or to a group is where we should start.

> We have found that it is crucial to start with sharing and then move on to nonjudg-
> mental kinds of responding before opening up to full criticism . . . the progression
> builds trust: trust in yourself and in the others you work with. You can't give good
> responses to writing or benefit from them except in a situation of trust.
>
> (Elbow & Belanoff 1989)

They acknowledge that we benefit from writing that remains private. It is often the case that freewriting remains unshared. Many teachers keep a private journal. However, all teachers' writing groups include the opportunity to share with no response other than the subtle reactions of your listeners. Elbow (2012) puts it like this:

> It turns out that we learn most about writing with our mouths and our ears. With
> our mouths we *feel* how our words and phrases and sentences work. With our ears
> we *hear* how our words sound – and also the words of others. What's nice is that
> this learning is *physical*, it occurs quickly *and without teaching*.

In *Vernacular Eloquence* (2012), Peter Elbow discusses further the power of simply reading aloud as a means of revising. In voicing our own words, we come to own them. We hear, quickly, where they sound strongest and where the weak points are. Reading aloud is a form of publishing. It is fundamental to revision and the development of organisation, musicality and even punctuation. The writer may read aloud in an empty room, but reading to at least one other and hearing his own words and those of others, will attune the ear and strengthen the other self. This simple sharing prepares us to find out how readers respond to our writing, which opens up for us its possibilities. It is good to hear how different readers respond and in a group all should take responsibility to do so. Try not, as a group leader, to feel bound to make the first, or only response. You should be one voice amongst many. In the first instance, though, it may be your responsibility to introduce some of the ways in which we can respond. Thanking writers for reading can have a great impact. One teacher spoke eloquently of the power of the words 'thank you'. Those two words acknowledge that what people are writing is important. It is an affirmation, which is where response should begin.

How might I respond in writing?

Some writing groups have benefitted from posting their writing on a closed VLE. Be aware that it is hard to persuade people to do so and when they do, you need to make sure that they receive a response. Their pleasure and relief when you do can be palpable.

> When I posted my extract onto the forum, I felt nauseous for several hours. . . .
> The euphoria (don't think I am exaggerating) when I received Simon's reply lasted

all day; I was so elated that he had read it. Not because I thought my writing was good; far, far from it, actually whether he thought it was good or not didn't matter at all, but because someone had read what I wrote, **accepted** it and made a comment. . . . everyone remarked on what a good mood I was in!

(Secondary teacher)

The first thing to do is to engage with the writer.

Read and believe. Engage with what the writer is saying and acknowledge that in your reply. What does this writer know? Try and build on what they say.

Learn from the writer.

Think carefully about what you know and what is most useful to share.

Ask one or two questions but not too many. Questions can signal to the writer what the reader is interested in and what is not so clear.

Offer some of your own ideas without being overpowering. I wonder . . . is a useful sentence starter. Acknowledge what the writer has shown you.

Don't say too much. Try to avoid a detailed analysis of what you think the writing is about and a rundown of your view of the style. Light touch. Light touch.

Try to: affirm what has been written; observe, or ask about how the text was arrived at or where the writer thinks it is going. Answer questions the writer themselves have asked of you.

- Think about these options for sharing and responding:

  - the whole text or a part of it? Sometimes we just read one sentence each.
  - immediately after a group exercise or later?
  - whole group, small groups or pairs?
  - new faces or familiar faces?
  - out loud or on paper or screen?
  - early or late drafts?

- Allow space for writers to share **only when ready**. Whilst too much emphasis on sharing can encourage showmanship, it is worth encouraging more reluctant sharers because they discover great pleasure in reading their work aloud.
- Don't rush to give detailed critiques. Know that simply reading aloud and being aware of the audience response has an impact.
- Peter Elbow (1989) says that as readers and as writers we are '**always right and always wrong**'. You benefit most if you read, and listen. As a reader, you can be sure of your perceptions but can never see the whole experience. As a writer you are always right because you are in charge of your writing but cannot quarrel with your reader's experience. You must be 'simultaneously sure of yourself and humble'.
- The simplest response is thanks. Listeners may ask the reader to slow down or to speak more clearly if they can't understand.
- Listeners – don't worry whether you like or don't like something, get engaged. Believe. Then try to sum up in a sentence or two what you feel the writer is *getting*

at. 'It seems that you begin with . . . The main thing I noticed . . . ' Don't give any suggestions about the writing itself.

- When you are responding, place the emphasis on how you experienced it rather than trying to fix it. If there are differences of perception, it is up to the writer to sort those out through their writing.
- Responses might focus on the process: *'Where did this writing come from? Which parts came easily? Which parts are you pleased with/would you like comment on? Where do you plan to take this writing?'*
- Responses might focus on sharing/discussing **content**. Sometimes readers have questions, which are helpful to the writer.
- Responses which **live alongside** the writer, withholding judgment, listening to the writer's distinctive voice, are often helpful.

  - Say which words, phrases and ideas you found interesting, puzzling or surprising.
  - Say what feelings or thoughts the writing evoked in you. This could be how it echoed your own experience, empathy for characters, what you felt at different points.
  - Say what images/pictures/sounds/textures/memories came to you when you read/listened to the writing.
  - Invite writers to ask their audience to think about a problem they are trying to solve in their writing.

References

Andrews, R. & Smith, A. (2011) *Developing Writers: Teaching and Learning in the Digital Age.* Maidenhead: Open University Press.

Britton, J. in Pradl, G.M. (ed.) (1982) *Prospect and Retrospect Selected Essays of James Britton.* Montclair NJ: Boynton/Cook.

Elbow, P. (1989) *Writing Without Teachers.* New York, Oxford: Oxford University Press.

Elbow, P. (2000) *Everyone Can Write: Essays Toward a Hopeful Theory of Writing and Teaching Writing.* New York, Oxford: Oxford University Press.

Elbow, P. (2012) *Vernacular Eloquence: What Speech Can Bring to Writing.* New York, NY: Oxford University Press.

Elbow, P. & Belanoff, P. (1989) *Sharing and Responding.* New York, NY: Random House.

Heard, G. (1989) *For the Good of the Earth and the Sun Teaching Poetry.* Portsmouth NH: Heinemann.

McKay, F. (1987) Chapter 6 'Roles and Strategies in College Writing Conferences.' In Bissex, G.L. & Bullock, Richard H. *Seeing for Ourselves: Case-study Research by Teachers of Writing.* Portsmouth, NH: Heinemann Educational Books, Inc.

Murray, D.M. (1982) 'The Listening Eye.' In *Learning by Teaching.* Montclair, NJ: Boynton Cook.

Rooke, J. (2012) *Transforming Writing Final Evaluation Report.* London: Esmee Fairbairn Foundation.

Chapter 9

Writing in different spaces

> I'm looking for a more intimate place with words that are planted, watered and talked about in spaces where people have invented warmth and twilight cosiness of friends meeting for tea.
>
> (Secondary teacher)

Choosing to meet and write in spaces other than a classroom holds many possibilities. Teachers report that children respond very positively to writing in a different setting. The greater freedom of the open air, gallery or historic house allows individuals to find spaces and ideas that suit them. Many current teachers' writing groups meet in public spaces. The pattern of the meeting is generally quite simple. The group gathers, often in the café. Sometimes a small task is given whilst people arrive. We might collect words or catch snatches of conversation. Then there is time for a short writing exercise and some sharing. A longer exercise may build on the initial activity or anticipate something that can be found in the space. Time is given for individuals to write. An hour will do. Finally, the group returns to the meeting place and the chance to hear what each other has been writing.

At their very best, places beyond the classroom offer writers a different perspective for their writing. The choice of location can make quite a difference to the way writing happens. A group probably needs to try out different places to discover what works for them. Sometimes the space can be overwhelming. There can be a sense of walking into a giant writing prompt that offers too much choice or which insists on a particular, and potentially oppressive, way of viewing the world. A group leader should think about how they might negotiate the space.

The suggestions made here are aimed at the adult writer. However, teachers' experiences of writing in different spaces have prompted them to take young writers to different locations and to discover how especially liberating that can be for them. Here is a London teacher and her Year 11 pupils reflecting on the experience:

> The Year 11 students are more reticent initially but once they become involved in their writing they take the stimuli and subvert them, making them their own. This was particularly true when I replicated a Writers' Meeting by taking them to the local history museum. Its contents are spectacularly uninspiring but despite this the

class colonised the building, each of them finding their own little space and view-point to write from. Afterwards, I asked them about the experience, and amongst the comments were:

> It's good to just get out of the classroom. How do you expect us to be inspired when we just have to stare at the same boring walls every lesson?
>
> It was great being able to sit on the floor and stretch out. Most of the time in lessons, because I'm so tall the furniture is really uncomfortable for me, so after the first twenty minutes, I'm just concentrating on not getting pins and needles.
>
> It felt different, being out of the classroom, I just wanted to write more. My head felt clearer.
>
> I liked the fact that there were no rules, I could write what I wanted to.
>
> One small thing that made a difference was that there were no clocks, and no teachers standing over you telling you how long you've got left.
>
> It didn't really feel like work. It was inventing stories.
>
> Listening to other people's writing made me think more about my own and want to go back to it, and finish it.

Here we provide some ways of thinking generally about writing on location:

Writing scavenger hunts

Scavenger hunts rose out of the desire to prompt writing about place that was in some way unexpected. They require writers to look in different ways and to interpret both the scavenger list and the location. They are based on the idea of a literal scavenger hunt in which you are asked to collect objects – a stone, a feather, something that would fit in a matchbox and so on. In a writing scavenger hunt, the list is rather less literal and the collection is written down rather than collected in a bag or box. The more we have worked with scavenger hunts, the more we have seen their many possibilities.

A writing scavenger allows for the inclusion of more abstract ideas than a conventional hunt and invites the writer to interpret the list in ways that suit them. Think about the ways in which your hunt can prompt the writer to look closely, to interpret, to look in ways that surprise them.

Scavenger hunt

Collect these items in writing. You may record them in any way you wish. Try and catch the details. Aim to collect them from one place.

- something grey
- something contained
- a gleam
- something high up

- something hidden
- a silence
- a corner
- an unexpectedness
- a sound made by a machine
- an opening
- no more than eleven consecutive words marked on something other than paper
- a swooping

You may choose a particular emphasis; invite writers to think about the narrative of a place or to use it as a springboard for their own story. You may wish to imagine the space as the setting for a known story, children especially like this: where might the treasure have been buried? Is there evidence that the wolf has passed by? The scavenger hunt becomes a hunt for a story trail in a real location. You could draw attention to certain aspects of the space: something golden; something rough; something glimpsed from the corner of the eye; something sour; a brush stroke; a trace.

You can see how easy it is to make up your own suggestions. The request for found text brings other people's words into the writing and can send writers to look at street furniture, official notices and the different voices of graffiti, greengrocer's labels, tombstones. Another item might invite the abstract: fear, loneliness, hope, things that might lie under the surface of a place. Prompts such as 'something hidden' or 'something that once was here' invite speculation and encourage storytelling.

Once the collection is made you can find that you may wish to write in a way that includes them all or that one or two things in particular have taken your interest. You might elaborate on one item, compose a detailed list or find yourself writing extended prose about two or three connected items.

We have successfully used scavenger hunts in places rich in detail and association and those that seem very unpromising. One colleague used the idea with A level students visiting Spitalfields, transforming it into a treasure hunt. She reduced the number of items on the list and expanded the media for recording and making to include drawing, photography, film and audio files. Students found their treasures using a small viewfinder cut from card. They described what they saw, using the viewfinder several times in the same place. They developed narratives, expanded into reflection and argument, shaped the poetic.

Collections

Museums and galleries house collections. Inside or out we can make our own word collections and, crucially, connections that can lead to fiction and non-fiction. The collection becomes the structure which underpins the composition. Most people will choose their own categories. Here are some: a collection of shoes/feet; eyes; jewellery; remnants; hands and gloves; joints and hinges – knees, elbows, hinged lids; hats/ hairdos; distant things; tiny things . . . Another form of collecting might involve a **chain of**

associations. Start anywhere with something that catches your attention. Follow it with something that links:

> the eyes of the man in the portrait look at the painting of a child opposite, she is dressed in pale blue, echoed by the blue eyes of the portrait next to her and those blue eyes remind me of my mother who loves flowers and look at these flowers in the background of this painting, neat and pale like this young woman walking through the gallery . . .

You get the idea. You may not wish to record what you notice in that way. It is the chain of connections that might prompt the piece of writing.

List ten things is a popular idea from the Scottish Poetry Library website (http:// www.spl.org.uk/about/index.html). Choose a painting, or use a postcard, and write a list of ten things: ten things the sitter is thinking; ten things Mrs Andrews would like to say to Mr Andrews; ten animals you can see or ten that you imagine in the space.

Listening

Close your eyes and experience the place through its sounds. Open your eyes and relocate. Listen again. Or simply move through the space with attention to sounds alone. How are the sounds made? What do they suggest? Can you write the place through evoking sound alone? Is it possible to write a soundscape, the soundtrack to a film, a narrative where sound plays a major part?

Looking

Lists can prompt figurative ways of looking. It is useful, especially outside, to redirect one's literal gaze. The simplest provocation is 'to look closely'. Inside or out, careful observational writing can be interesting. The prompt to 'describe a detail you hadn't noticed before' forces you back to the object. Another simple device is to look 'near and far'. Notice and describe something close up, and then move away and see how it looks at a distance – or vice versa: "on closer inspection I noticed . . .". Something that is pleasurable **outdoors** is to have a set of prepositions or instructions for looking. These can be handed out, scattered on the floor or given to individuals to use on their own. Walking together through a wood, stop at various points and ask writers to choose a viewpoint from a selection: 'up close', 'underneath', 'below', 'high up', and to write using that viewpoint. We have enjoyed the work of the artist, Richard Long, whose walking and making is often governed by self-imposed patterning (http://www. richardlong.org/). A white light walk began with red leaves of a Japanese maple and ended with violet wild cyclamen at 72 miles. In the Brecon Beacons, Long built seven cairns in the course of a four-day walk, and he records these: a cairn built where a raven flew off, a cairn built near sheep bones, and so on (Long 2002). This walking and looking, the marking of spaces, has provoked us to look and write in different ways, even in the familiar landscape of where we meet regularly.

Meetings outdoors are dependent on the weather. One group's favourite place by a river was enhanced by autumn sunshine, which, one writer observed 'may have contributed to the emotion of the meeting'. Here is another writer, returning to a shared space. She says it is 'a bit autobiographical and a bit not'.

> I sit in the closeness of my children; loving, demanding and creating worlds out of everything. We stood, holding hands in a circle in a dip on the hillside. I told them it was where the rainbow colours landed and they believed. A butterfly passes, they ask will it be in my story? And then peace. A writes, wants to be like me. B waits for her turn with the pencil and so picks flowers and grass and snail shells for her collecting bag. They try to read my words on the page. It's everyone's right to be private sometimes I say, moving away a little. I need to write myself right again.
>
> I came here before, inspired and befriended by writers, and I looked for different ways to be myself. I found that when you stretch the boundaries there is both pleasure and pain. Split myself in two? Old crow. Young dancer. I thought that I could double, could share and increase. I thought I could go back. All the rainbow colours of my heart . . . that's what I say now to the children as I explain the different ways I love them.
>
> Split myself in two? Result, I'm lessened. Less whole. Half life. Diminishing returns.
>
> [. . .]
>
> It's strange the way we always bring ourselves as we are to the landscape, and we look for healing there, even though we've lost our sense of connection with the land. Patchwork beauty sown together with lines of urban conquest. Soft green slopes, trumpeting sounds of trains and a thin thread of motorway beetles shining in the distance. And I look at my wrongs and I look at my chances and I contemplate again time passing, and I ponder as I watch my children searching again for the exact spot where the end of the rainbow lands. Will there be a crock of gold? Which hill does the other end land on? Can you find the edge of rain?

Conversations

Museums and galleries are filled with images and objects which can prompt personal writing or open up avenues of thought. Consider writing in the voice of an object, addressing it directly or striking up a conversation. Teachers have written in the voice of a Chinese porcelain pillow and of a sturdy, hobnailed child's shoe from first or second century London; answered back to the throne of weapons and meditated on a stone sculpture of lovers. Here is a piece written by a secondary teacher, followed by her reflection on how it arose.

Victory

About victory, they were never wrong, the Ancient Greek Olympians. Or something like that.

I look at this one, standing before me, haughty-eyed and jaunty-hipped. Right down through to the marbled bones of his arrogant legs, he knows what it is to be one of life's winners. Even here, in this bright room, two and a half thousand years later, he has it, whatever 'it' may be. The X-factor. A winning quality. And his is preserved in stone for tourists and schoolchildren alike.

The stone fabric tunic folds around his sweaty trunk. The toil is over, his race is won. Pert buttocks somehow give movement to the lifeless marble. What he's wearing, tied loosely round his waist, the little card tells me is his 'xystis'.

Well. My xystis is my apron. My chariot is a pram. My existence is my children. They swarm around me, now, in the museum, and I am scared that they will touch something, knock something, break something. They are young things, bright and vibrant against the white antiquity.

It has been a long day traipsing round London with three under sixes, trailing blankets, snot and the remains of lunch. Though I read that ancient chariot races were also gruelling events.

And when we get home, and they finally sleep soundly tonight – after the tantrum on the train and the bedtime battles, I too become, momentarily, the victor. I am the winner who has taken all, finishing with the contentment of clinging fingers of a child and a kiss goodnight. My chalice is held aloft and I sip greedily of Sangiovese. My sigh is deep and satisfied.

But hooded eyes, aching hips and knackered knees form *my* victory stance.

And as for pert buttocks? Not a chance.

Tomorrow there will be another race. I limber up.

This piece of writing was the first time I 'shared'. We had met at the British Museum and gone off to write something inspired by one of the exhibits. I was struck by the confident pose of the 'Motya Charioteer' and transported to the thrill of the chariot race. My own difficult and dangerous sport seemed to be the raising of my children, and I enjoyed combining the two ideas. People laughed at 'arrogant legs' and at the 'pert buttocks' bit when I read it out and I found that very uplifting. I haven't looked back. There's a definite structure to this piece of writing as well as internal rhyme. I think there is a poem in there, somewhere, that I might come back to one day. The use of an object, in this case a sculpture, as an inspiration really took me in an unexpected direction and I have returned to that since, both in my own writing and in the classroom.

(Secondary teacher)

Close attention to an object, a portrait or a piece of furniture can be the starting point for fiction, by suggesting a character, puzzle or event. Sometimes an object will give rise to personal memories. An exhibition can invite different approaches. We responded to the Living Landscapes show at the Sainsbury Centre for Visual Arts (SCVA) in Norwich by creating and writing on paper landscape sculptures, some of which became the setting for film animation. In this case careful preparation was made for the visit. Sometimes writers find a theme through objects. We have mentioned the writer who engaged with issues of feminism through her interest in textiles: embroideries, tapestries, fashion.

The writing was an exploration of ideas rather than memoir. Museums can feed such an interest with new perspectives and information. Writers find that, alongside the objects themselves, they weave in museum notes and even the voices of other visitors.

Texts

Whilst some galleries provide plenty of text, it can be interesting to introduce words that push a writer's thoughts. Site-specific words inhabit and enliven individual pieces of writing. The searching of related texts for words and phrases can introduce language that the writer may not have otherwise thought of. We have used maps and nature writing in a gallery, plant and bird identification books on the Chilterns, extracts from *A History of the World in 100 Objects* (MacGregor 2010) in the British Museum. Sometimes writers scour the texts themselves, making a collection or following a lead. Extracts as a starter for freewriting, can reorientate thoughts. Sometimes the most unprepossessing texts can yield interesting writing. In preparation for a workshop at Christchurch Mansion in Ipswich, we cut phrases from a very dull introduction to the building and glued them to tiny tags. Writers used them as personal labels before choosing one item to write about. The placing of the label, the words in relation to the object shifted how writers thought about the house and its artefacts. Introduction of text challenges ideas and expands the lexicon.

New spaces take writers out of their familiar environment. A group leader can help writers to find a starting point or to gain the most from the particular setting. However, most of us simply welcome some time to write and these public places provide that time and space, with the promise of a trusted audience with whom to share at the end of it.

A special issue of *Writing in Education*, Volume 54 NAWE, *Writing on Location*, is devoted to site specific ideas derived from the British Library's *Literature in Context* project.

References

Long, R. (2002) *Walking the Line*. London: Thames & Hudson.

MacGregor, N. (2010) *A History of the World in 100 Objects*. London: Allen Lane.

NAWE. 'Writing on Location.' In *Writing in Education*, Volume 54. NAWE. Retrieved from: http://www.nawe.co.uk/DB/current-wie-edition/editions/writing-on-location.html.

Scottish Poetry Library website (http://www.spl.org.uk/about/index.html)

Chapter 10

Reading into writing and back again

> Students who don't read are always writing with one hand tied behind their backs.
>
> (Secondary teacher)

Writers frequently acknowledge their indebtedness to their reading, to the writers who have gone before them. A. S. Byatt, quoted in Barrs and Cork (2001), asserts her belief that it is good reading that makes possible good writing. It is a truism to say that those who read well, write well, but we tend to be less clear how this might be so. If the teaching of writing is under-researched, the links between reading and writing are explored even less. James Britton (1989) suggested that it would seem a perverse regime that attempted to separate the teaching of speaking and of listening, yet we continue to make that precise division between reading and writing. Well-meaning attempts to articulate characteristics of genres have not necessarily improved children's writing, rather given them a series of rules and tricks to be performed. We need to have a clearer idea of what kind of reading informs writing and how teachers can best provide that experience for young writers.

> I don't remember learning, or being taught, to write, but have no memory of ever *not* writing. Writing and reading were entwined – my own comics and stories paid loving homage to 'The Beano' and Blyton. . . . Recently, I came across work saved from my NQT year. I was so much more willing to experiment then. What changed? External pressures: the Framework, SATs, league tables, the C/D borderline, GCSE changes. Or maybe it was me, becoming less willing to take 'risks' over the years. The literacy strategy, which had won me over with its sales pitch as a way to liberate working class students, seemed to throw the baby out with the bathwater. I remember an advisor questioning 'what on earth were we doing having library lessons where children *just read*' – but I wrote as a child *because I read*. There were some brilliant resources from central government, I still look to them and see all the best intentions, but levels and targets became ends in themselves, and the SATs were sheer, reductive, misery.
>
> (Secondary teacher)

In her preface to *The Reader in the Writer,* (Barrs & Cork 2001), Margaret Meek suggests that those 'whose reading appears in their writing of *continuous* text have discovered a different kind of consciousness'. She says it is the tunes and rhythm of the text that they acquire first, what Francine Prose (2007) believes she learned 'by osmosis'. Carol Fox's study (1993) of the oral storytelling of preschool children unfolds the complexities of their spoken narratives. She shows how children who are not yet independent readers, but who have been read to from the earliest years, harness that written language in their imaginative verbal play. The oral narratives which she analyses embody the forms and language of written texts and show how children have absorbed the vocabulary, rhythms and syntactic structures of the texts they have listened to. She makes a powerful argument for the power of narrative as a means of learning and exploration of thought, regarding it as an inclusive form rather than narrowly fictional. In hearing stories read or told, or in watching television or film, children come to understand how narratives work and acquire a particular knowledge of language. Teachers need to know about the texts that children bring with them to school and to see how children draw on them to fuel their narrative explorations (Dyson 1997).

Fox observed the difference between children's own narratives and two examples of children playing at 'reading'. That is, their reading of an imagined scheme book had none of the rhythm and grace of their storytelling. 'Each word is stabbed out separately and her expressive skills disappear . . . Sundari is showing how she perceives reading is done through the stiff, unyielding texts of the reading scheme. It is clear that the notion of story, imaginative play, phonological patterns, rhythms and rhymes and topsy-turvies have to be abandoned in the forms of language used in the scheme' (Fox 1993: 192). Perhaps we learn first about writing, through the ear. We need to be sure that all children hear many texts read aloud. As writers mature, we can make more explicit the techniques that writers use. We should learn more about what teachers can do to facilitate the connections that young writers may make between reading and writing. Barrs and Cork (2001) have already made an important contribution to our understanding of this and have illuminated what that relationship might be.

Teachers reading

Most teachers are skilled readers. Their first, and sometimes inhibiting, love is of the written word. They are usually aware of which writers have influenced and do influence them, and have experience of that echoing of style that can come unbidden to one's own writing. It makes them skilled readers of young writers' texts.

In teachers' writing groups we use reading in many ways. We find that close attention to text during a session can have a direct impact on how we write. The perusal of cookery books and restaurant reviews brought new vocabulary and the desire to parody to a session spent food writing. The discovery of dialect words for landscape made us look with new eyes at a familiar scene. Those of us who write in museums often find the language of guidebooks and labelling shapes what we write. The instruction to find and record 'no more than eleven consecutive words written on something other than paper' not only makes us look more carefully, but introduces other voices. Similarly, small tags, printed with fragments of prose, not only require a new way of looking but bring unfamiliar phrases to the writer's attention. We become aware of the many different textual tunes we know well, and those that are less familiar. It seems important to recognise the range of texts that adults and children bring with them and to think about the texts that can expand the writing repertoire. We think that it is repeated readings, both silent and aural, that introduce the rhythms of the text to the writer, rather than dissection and rules, but this needs further exploration.

We often use text, most frequently a poem, as a starting point. The poem is read aloud and rarely seen on the page. It offers a particular viewpoint, a pattern of language, the rhythm and music of its author. Writers pick up the offering of the original text in different ways. There is rarely an expectation that the text should serve as a strict model. What does seem important, in a group, is the reading aloud. Ursula Le Guin (1998) emphasises this in her excellent book on writing narrative, *Steering the Craft*. In a series of exercises designed to develop skills, Le Guin commands us to read aloud extracts which exemplify the focus skill. Her emphasis throughout the book is on the sound of writing: 'The sound of the language is where it all begins and what it all comes back to'. In response to a reading of Le Guin's litany of place names, one teacher remembered Australia:

Gorgeous (Colours of Australia)

We drove North to Brewarrina
Narayan and I
Past Orange and Dubbo
Out west of the wop-wops
To the back of Bourke.
Where 'blackfellas' sat in the shade,
(Sharing a bottle of Bundaberg Rum).

Some sizeable brown women
With eyes of treacle
And generous smiles,
Spirited me away for
Secret women's business
Back at the bowls club.

Insisting I was their sister
And introducing me to all
The Aunties and cousins
And quick, bright, beautiful,
Big eyed children, who in turn
Led me to their leader –

In the run down, rusted
Red corrugated metal hut,
Where there was ping-pong
And dancing and Coca-Cola
Cooling in the esky, until
It was time to return to

The Brewarrina Hotel
For the six o'clock swill
And escape from the
Hot red, dry red, dust red
Town. And it's down with
A schoon and some stares

From the hard baked,
Red necked, booted and
Capped men, leaning
Wearily on the
Smooth brown mahogany
Of the public bar.

She writes:

> *I immediately thought of a journey through New South Wales. Initially I intended to list as many wonderful aboriginal place names as possible, but as I wrote, it was the memory of the people I met rather than the names, that struck me as 'being gorgeous'. I originally wrote it as a piece of continuous prose, but on reading it aloud to the group, the natural rhythm of the writing was so obvious that I later organised it into stanzas with very little editing. . . . I loved the way it sounded when read aloud.*

The reading of the original text and subsequent sharing of outcomes expands our writing repertoires. Francine Prose, suggests that there are two elements to the reading of texts in ways that inform writing:

> In the ongoing process of becoming a writer, I read and reread the authors I most loved. I read for pleasure, first, but also more analytically, conscious of style, of diction, of how sentences were formed and information was being conveyed, how the writer was structuring a plot, creating characters, employing detail and dialogue.
>
> (Prose 2007: 3)

In *Reading Like a Writer*, Prose provides the kind of close reading of fiction she suggests a writer should undertake, beginning with the significance of word choice through to a final chapter she calls 'Reading for Courage' which is a defence against self-doubt.

It is a book that informs the writer who has written or aspires to write something and who seeks the reading that may answer some questions.

> Reading because you have written something and now you are looking to see how others do it; reading because you want to write something ditto; reading because you have come up against a problem; how do others solve it? Reading to shift one-self out of a rut. Reading to find a starting point. Reading for the sheer pleasure of it.

A writing group is likely to discuss the reading that has influenced individual pieces and the texts they are reminded of. They often share recommendations. Once teachers begin to write together and to hear each other's writing, they find they may well read differently:

> NWP has affected me as a reader. I now read more poetry, old and new. I find I have a greater depth of understanding and frequently the words speak to me more clearly. It gives me more pleasure.
>
> (Primary teacher)

Reading is important for writing teachers both for personal and professional development. Their experience is as adult writers. Their experience as teachers allows them to apply what they learn through writing for themselves to their teaching practice. Frank Smith (1984) suggests that 'the learner learns through *reading* like a writer to *write* like a writer'. However, unless children are placed in a position to do so they are much less likely to make the connections. It is the teacher who writes herself, and who reads like a writer, who is well placed to foster the child writer-reader. The value of reading like a writer was explored in the Teaching Reading and Writing Links (TRAWL) project (Corden 2001). Children developed meta-cognitive awareness through close readings of texts and the encouragement to talk about the choices they were making as writers.

> Teacher-researchers involved in the TRAWL project believe that, with support from the teacher; providing models, demonstrating and drawing attention to the features of texts, and through group discussion, children can develop their awareness of how texts are constructed. Children can become familiar with the devices used by successful authors and encouraged to adopt them in their own writing. However, it is not our intention to encourage a formulaic production of texts where children 'write to order'. On the contrary, we wish to develop children's strategic repertoires so they can make conscious choices and take control over their own writing.
>
> (Corden 2001)

Of greatest interest is the elegant research reported in *The Reader in the Writer* (Barrs and Cork 2001). The project took as its starting point the assumption with which we began this chapter – that what children write reflects the nature and quality of their reading – and set out to test this assumption. Six Year 5 teachers spent a year working with texts in ways which made specific connections between reading and writing. Teachers used a variety of approaches, including reading aloud, drama, close readings and well-supported discussion, writing in the first person, writing extensions of the shared text. The project established a clear link between children's involvement with literary texts and their development as writers. One striking finding was the positive impact the work had on the two English as an Additional Language (EAL) writers in the sample, one of whom was a fluent speaker and the other an inexperienced user of English.

The Reader in the Writer project moved us well beyond the hunch that reading plays an important part in becoming a good writer. It develops understanding of how teachers consciously develop the links between reading and writing in using whole texts. We return to 'the tune of the language'. Just as the preschool children in Fox's study were attuned to written language through the ear so these older children became apprentices to experienced writers, through the body and through close readings. The teachers in the project played a crucial role as mediators of text and as knowledgeable readers of children's writing. Teachers gifted texts to children through their readings, and through careful interrogation of what was written. Reading aloud helps the writer to hear their own writing more acutely and to develop their inner voice. Where reading aloud is commonplace, writers become accustomed to listening carefully to their own writing and that of others. Close discussion of rich, polysemic texts enabled the children in the study to become comfortable with the multiple meanings of any single text and to become increasingly conscious of writing for a reader. In adult writing groups, reading aloud and the sharing of personal reading arises naturally.

Readings on teaching and on writing

The Reader in the Writer reminds us just how complex a task writing is. In order to teach it well the teacher needs to be knowledgeable and increasingly experienced. The teachers in the Centre for Literacy in Primary Education (CLPE) project had different strengths and these were reflected in their varying approaches. We do not have to know everything. However, we do believe that teachers should read in order to inform their teaching. A teachers' writing group can support such reading. It provides a forum for discussion and the development of shared understandings. The Buckinghamshire group was encouraged to read articles and chapters from a range of sources. Teachers shared their readings of novels, poetry and narrative non-fiction amongst other things. What proved very useful were the digested reads that you can now find on the NWP UK website. Some readings have a strong impact on practice and become a part of the thinking of teacher-writers who are inspired by them. Readings with a pedagogical focus and those that are about writing both have their place in writing groups. Peter Elbow, David Morley and Kenneth Koch were all popular in one group; Kate Pahl, Georgia Heard and Ursula Le Guin favoured in another. The annotated reading list (Chapter 20) includes texts currently most popular amongst teacher-writers.

References

Barrs, M. & Cork, V. (2001) *The Reader in the Writer*. London: Centre for Language in Primary Education.

Britton, J. (1989) 'Writing and Reading in the Classroom.' In Dyson, A. H. (ed.) *Collaboration through Writing and Reading*. Urbana, Illinois: NCTE.

Corden, R. (2001) 'Teaching Reading-writing Links (TRAWL project).' In *Literacy*, 35(1), 37–40.

Dyson, A. H. (1997) *Writing Superheroes: Contemporary Childhood, Popular Culture, and Classroom Literacy*. New York & London: Teachers College Press.

Fox, C. (1993) *At the Very Edge of the Forest: The Influence of Literature on Storytelling by Children*. London: Cassell.

Le Guin, U. K. (1998) *Steering the Craft: Exercises and Discussions on Story Writing for the Lone Navigator or the Mutinous Crew*. Portland Oregon: The Eight Mountain Press.

Prose, F. (2007) *Reading Like a Writer: A Guide for People Who Love Books and for Those Who Want to Write Them*. New York: First Harper Perennial.

Smith, F. (1984) *Reading Like a Writer*. Reading: Reading Reading Centre.

Chapter 11

Reflecting on writing

> From a pedagogical point of view, techniques of improving writing will include practice in writing by the very teachers who are teaching it. In other words, English teachers, will need to be *accomplished writers* in themselves, not only of literary and fictional genres but in informational and argumentative genres too. They will not only be able to produce final products in this range of genres ('Here's one I made earlier . . .'), but also **to reflect on and model the processes of writing** in the classroom.
>
> (Andrews & Smith 2011: 10–11, our emphasis)

What do you know about yourself as a writer?

Writing ability develops in the drive to shape meaning. By engaging in the act of writing one is learning to write. It is not a skill that can be taught or learned independently of the need to do so. This is one of the reasons why teachers writing together can make such a powerful contribution to professional development. It is the capacity to 'reflect on and model the processes of writing in the classroom' that is distinctive about writing teachers. The kind of meta-cognitive awareness that arises from private reflection and communal discussion informs both the development of the writer in the teacher, and the teacher of writing. It informs thinking about how we teach, the nature of the writing environment and the kinds of activity we expect from those we teach. It prompts us to think deeply about the writing process in ways that inform day-to-day practice. The evidence in this chapter is drawn mainly from long-standing writing groups where there are opportunities to reflect on development over time.

Teachers are interested in what writers have to say about how their writing happened and where it might go. In listening to the writing of others we can sometimes feel daunted, but we also learn more about writing and about the kind of writer we would like to be.

> As well as the drive to write, NWP has encouraged me to experiment. I also seem to have lost the worry that everything I write has to work.
>
> (Buckinghamshire teacher)

> I write more and my writing now is a bit more 'free' and I am not so hasty to cross out and add. I have been surprised at how much more 'courage' I have to write things down and leave them now. (For pupils, this has been the key to 'helping'

them write). Now when I start writing, I am conscious that I should trust that out-pouring a little bit more and it is ok if it is not perfect, or as perfect as you would like. This has meant that I have had the nerve to use images and styles I would never have used before as I would have felt them to be too obvious or the oppo-site, too outlandish. A big thing has been how not to 'try' to be a writer and just convey what you want to say. (Still have trouble not over complicating language) and I am learning that the power of simplicity lies in its honesty. The reason for these 'insights'? A trusted and reassuring audience. Which leads me on to the next important change in my writing habits. This has to do with editing.

I have found that having an audience has opened my eyes to the process of edit-ing. I realise that my editing was ruthless, never-ending, but more importantly it consisted of adding and embellishing, over complicating, not cutting. I don't think I ever did really cut; I think I just replaced with a preferred alternative. Having an audience through NWP has been the most fantastic experience, and it is because it has given me the confidence to write and share in the first place, but also because when I have read the responses, I can see my writing through those eyes and I now write with those comments in mind. For me, that has meant not over editing and more importantly, editing now means much more cutting than correcting and decorating.

(Buckinghamshire teacher)

Teachers who were part of the Buckinghamshire TAW group captured something of their journeys as writers by regularly responding to a series of prompts we called 'My Writing Now'. They are adapted from David Morley's 'Writing Game: Who are you?' (2007). Teachers responded four times to these prompts over the course of two years.

This adaptation of David Morley's provocation is one you might like to use:
    We would like you to write a statement about yourself as a writer at this moment. The writing is both for your personal use and as part of the wider group's reflec-tion on the process of writing as a teacher. The audience for this will be yourself, project leaders and, then, any other person you choose.

Aim: 'We write for many reasons; sometimes those reasons converge into writerly purpose. They might include a desire to play with language and/or form; share a part of yourself; describe an emotion; communicate with the world; bring a character to life; express your opinion; or simply tell a story. We would like you to . . . . . . use this first statement as a measure of how far your creative thinking and reading has progressed. Please be honest with yourself. Do not pretend achievements or ways of speaking which are not yet your own, or with which you feel uncomfortable. Writers must be honest with themselves – except when they are writing.'

(Morley 2007: 37)

Use these prompts and suggestions to frame your writing. You do not have to address every point. Write what is important to you at this moment. Write quickly and without too much deliberation.

- Why do you write and how do you write?
- Are there pressures in your life which force you into writing silence?
- Are there impulses that help you, push you to write?
- What drives and what hinders you?
- Describe your current reasons and methods.
- Be sure to write about those writers who have influenced your thinking and direction.
- How can you improve your writing conditions and how can you just make the most of your current situation?
- What picture do you think those you teach have of you as a writer?
- What do you like most about writing? . . . and about what you have written?
- What is your wish for yourself as a writer in the coming year?
- What is your wish for yourself as a teacher of writing?
- Include one anecdote, – more if you are inclined – a story from the year that sums up something about writing and teaching writing that is important to you; that puzzles you; that is a moment of celebration.

Guilt and permissions

What prevents us from writing? Guilt comes high on the list so permission becomes an important element of the writing group. Fear of failure, for those with a good degree in English Literature, is great. Despite the desire, the stakes seem too high;

> That tension between wanting to write and the fear of being mediocre has haunted me for a long time. . . . If I can't be the next AS Byatt or even Kate Atkinson, I don't want to play.
>
> (Secondary teacher)

For others, an early experience of humiliation in connection with writing has had a lasting effect. It is possible to address this during initial teacher education. A PGCE student, in answer to the question, 'How would you describe yourself as a writer?' wrote, 'Reluctant', a single word, hunched on the page. She told us how, when she moved school at six years old, she took great care with the first story she wrote there, and thought she had done a good job. That story was torn up in front of the class because her handwriting was not joined – and in *that* class *everyone* wrote using a joined hand, something that the child had had no experience of. She chose to join the writing group and continued when she qualified.

Groups situated in universities and attached to Initial Teacher Education (ITE) courses are well-placed to catch the truly reluctant writer before they carry their crippled approach to writing into the classroom. Sometimes teachers join once they are qualified because they have identified their own need and are happy to return to a trusted setting. The teacher who acknowledged his own reluctance to write and joined the group six years ago continues to entertain and inspire us with his inventive ways of engaging his own reluctant writers. If the workshop is open, affirmative and real – that is, there is a genuine response to what people do, then a change happens to teachers' writing and to their teaching almost instantly. That word 'permission' comes up frequently. As this teacher writes, 'I felt empowered by the whole experience of 'being given permission' to write. It was a bit like falling in love.' For those who are interested and inclined to write, there is an almost immediate falling into writing.

However, soon after the first flush of pleasure, things can become more difficult. A single workshop can be enjoyed and then largely forgotten, or remembered with nostalgia. A longer term commitment draws attention to the difficulties and requires writer-teachers to confront them. Back to the guilt: 'Writing always feels self-indulgent.' (Buckinghamshire teacher). Are we not allowed to enjoy teaching or our own professional development?

> I love writing but I need pressure and deadlines to get me doing it (often have paralysing case of mother/teacher guilt that I "should be doing something else").
>
> (Primary teacher)

> Writing silence is caused for me sometimes by a sense of guilt. There can be so much school paperwork to do that I wonder what I am doing thinking about my own writing? There is often a feeling of being overwhelmed and thus not achieving anything. . . . I need to stop making excuses and simply write, not in the expectation that what I produce will be wonderful but understanding that nothing will be achieved if I don't actually place words on the paper. I begin to realise that one shouldn't try to find an empty week, day, hour but instead *consider writing important and just do it!*
>
> (Buckinghamshire teacher)

The requirement to write demanded by the project, and in the case of Buckinghamshire TAW, to post regularly on a VLE, made teachers think seriously about the demands of writing:

> I suppose I am a perfectionist and it is a fear of being imperfect that creates an enormous amount of hesitancy and self-doubt in my writing process. Before writing, I make a cup of coffee, I become engrossed in a poorly acted out sitcom (which isn't at all humorous!), I stare out of the window, I suck on the pen nib, I click incessantly on the top of the pen. I read and research around the subject. I procrastinate.

I run out of time. At the moment, I'm struggling to achieve what David Morley calls, "the skills of psychological sturdiness" that a writer needs to succeed.

(Primary teacher)

What came to be known as 'psycho-sturdiness' in the Buckinghamshire group became a major preoccupation as teachers struggled to make time for their own writing. Then they acknowledged the drudgery which many writers refer to, the sheer hard work of sitting down to get words on the page and they came to understand what writing meant for them. Part of this is about coming to terms with one's own writing.

TAW has changed me and my life in a way I fully expect to last . . . I do now write, I am addicted to my journals. . . . I love writing on trains and in museums and galleries . . . and I have learned how much more effective and satisfying it is to write about the tiny incident/thought/glance than something huge . . .

(Primary teacher)

I write more now because I have allowed it to become a habit and I have allowed it to be what it is, instead of judging my writing by what I think it ought to be. I still write sporadically in spite of nurturing the intention to become more disciplined, but at the moment I feel like I have to be accepting of that. If I waited for the moment of perfect organisation around my children, planning and marking to fit in writing, it would never happen. However, I do feel that I need to learn more discipline in order to achieve all the things I want to do.

I think that the habit of writing has allowed some pressures to lift. For example, in 'Mary's Story' . . . I let myself adopt a voice that represented ideas I felt were powerful and explored alternative mythologies and representations; I don't think I would have given myself that freedom before. Sometimes I feel silenced by what I see to be the repetitive nature of my ideas and writing, but I also think that if I write through that knot of an idea, I might untangle it and move beyond it.

I think the impulses that push me to write have changed subtlety because writing feels a more validated means of expression. Writing creates moments of reflection, captures moments of truth that I know will shift and change and alter, writing creates opportunities to express the different people that I am, and has actually made a real difference in the choices that I make and the richer life I feel I live. Maybe some of those elements would have evolved without NWP, but it seems a strong coincidence to me. I am much more aware of writing and what it brings me, and that has made me value the impulse to write more highly.

(Secondary teacher)

Writing the self

Writing is often, if not always, for the self. Perhaps that is where the sense of indulgence comes from. However, teachers come to feel the benefits of writing and to recognise its place in their lives and their responsibility towards themselves.

> I write. It is important to me and has become an integral part of who I am.
> And I want to write as a way of inhabiting my life more fully.
> A road back into myself.
>
> (Buckinghamshire teachers)

Teachers began to talk about the personal value of writing. They knew it made them feel good and began to see it as equally worthwhile as a session at the gym or a cross-country run. If that is true on a day-to-day basis, teachers see that although 'seismic shifts' in personal life can bring writing to a halt, writing can also help.

> I have been driven to write through difficult emotions and personal dilemmas, almost embarrassingly so, because of the perspective and healing that I feel as a result. I feel that I can 'write myself right'. I am hindered by time, by the fear I will reveal aspects of myself that I would normally keep hidden.
>
> (Secondary teacher)

We do need to recognise the part writing can play in exploring the personal and to recognise that it can afford us healing, allow us to settle ourselves somehow. Many teacher-writers begin by writing autobiographical pieces which have an important part to play in their development as writers.

Identities

Just as there are many ways to teach, so teachers find that there are many ways to write. This is discovered in the company of others. What is learned is integral to our writing and becomes the deep subject knowledge that will inform teaching. 'I have much more confidence in what I write. I know when it sounds good and when it says what I mean.'(Secondary teacher). It is our knowledge of writing and of ourselves as writers that we can, potentially, bring to teaching. Etienne Wenger argues that teachers, rather than taking on an identity defined by the institution, as upholders of curriculum demands, should '"represent" their communities of practice':

> for students, it is the kind of access to experience they need in order to feel connected to subject matter. This principle suggests that being an active practitioner with an authentic form of participation might be one of the most essential requirements for teaching.
>
> (Wenger 1998: 277)

Few writing teachers are published authors. Their experience of writing is likely to be nearer to that of their students. The writing group forms the community of practice that shapes the identity and does not expect anyone to be a prizewinning novelist. Writing teachers learn the affordances of writing.

Before the writing group I was someone who had a desire to write only ever in an isolated capacity and one who did not give enough time to writing. [It]. . . . has encouraged me to find the space to write not just in our writers' meetings but also outside of these, to share and discuss my writing for the first time and to begin to consider myself as being 'a writer'. It has had a hugely positive and influential impact on my own relationship with writing and the way in which I teach it.

(Secondary teacher)

Teachers do have reservations and they find ways through them:

I feel I am still one of the more reserved writers in our group. I still need a nudge to write. . . . I like writing when it's just for me and there are no worries about someone else reading it.

(Primary teacher)

TAW has not been a totally smooth pathway, ever moving onwards and upwards. I have had wobbles on the way:. . . . Can I actually write? Is it just pretentious rubbish? Everyone else is far better than me. . . . [group-facilitator] did convince me that I had a voice and something to say. That was comforting and consoling and I suppose in the end I began to believe it.

(Primary teacher)

We do not claim that it is easy (some of the difficulties are explored by Cremin & Baker). We do witness the benefits that teachers derive from writing themselves.

How do I write?

Teachers rethink what they do in the classroom in the light of what they learn about themselves and others.

I've been staring at the screen for the past five minutes trying to think of an answer to the question: How do you write? I'm not sure where it starts, mostly, I think, in daydreams. I carry ideas in my head for weeks sometimes before committing them to paper. Walking, driving, wandering around Tesco's, standing in the playground on duty . . . this is where the writing process starts. . . . Once the ideas have stewed, I have to lock myself away in a quiet place with my laptop and let rip.

(Secondary teacher)

I have developed a strange but exciting heightened awareness. Words and phrases jump out at me. Scenarios in the street become pieces of writing in my head. I see and think slightly differently; it has become easier to see the extraordinary in the ordinary. I have realised how the 'everyday' incidents make up most of our lives and as such they are important and can be powerful. Pre-TAW I would have opened my freezer and pondered as to whether to take out the trout or the quiche. Recently when I did this the line leapt into my head: 'there is a lone trout in my freezer', and these words stayed stubbornly with me until I sat down and wrote a few days later.

(Primary teacher)

I write, after much thought and deliberation, usually in a single setting. I organise thoughts and ideas in my head – trying sentences out, moving words around – before committing to paper. My writing can flow at times, and at other times is a staccato process of writing/thinking/writing/thinking, where both the pen and mind distance themselves from the paper. I tend to work best when there's a deadline as the adrenaline speeds up the thinking process, and will frequently leave writing assignments to the last possible moment. . . . I mostly write with a Biro onto an A4 notebook before transferring it to text. I edit and revise most of my work while transferring the writing from paper onto screen. I write sitting on the bed or at a bedside desk, sometimes in silence, sometimes with music – The Beatles, The Doors, The Eels. I generally write alone, although I have enjoyed writing collaboratively with NWP participants and children in my class.

(Primary teacher)

Firstly, difficulty in writing. Yes indeed. My approach is very chaotic; it isn't an approach at all. It just grows in all directions and is very messy. I tended to hide this and it made me feel that I really should not write at all, as surely writing was supposed to be an 'inspired flow'. Mine was (and is) a lengthy, hideously unstructured process with much crossing out and moving around and I was (and am) never happy with what I end up with. This stopped me writing many things, some things I wasn't even aware that I wished to write about – in fact, I was unaware how much it did stop. The barriers to writing are, I think, very complex, and in understanding what it is at a certain point that stops us or makes it hard, requires large amounts of honesty (maybe we will never really know).

(Secondary teacher)

I am now, after nearly two and a half years of writing meetings, much more prolific. I write for myself regularly, outside of the meetings. I now write a journal again, something that I haven't done for about twenty years, and have been bold enough to enter the odd short story competition. I write short and longer stories for my own children. On holiday last summer their bedtime story was written around 'adventures' during the day.

(Secondary teacher)

Two activities to prompt reflection on writing and the nature of writing

The writer: a natural history

Jill Krementz' (1996) book *The Writer's Desk* is a collection of photographs of writers writing. Each photograph is accompanied by a brief personal commentary by the writer. *The Guardian* newspaper published a similar series of photographs of writers' rooms with a commentary (http://www.theguardian.com/books/series/writersrooms). Krementz' collection of photographs includes images of writers standing, sitting in bed, even perched cross-legged on a kitchen worktop. Some writers are surrounded by books and papers, others' spaces are more austere.

Gather a list of questions that you would like to ask each other about writing. Draw up an interview schedule from your favourites. Here are some examples:

Where do you write . . . and where is your favourite place to write?
Do you like to write amidst noise or silence? What kind?
What do you like to drink when you are writing?
Where is your favourite place to buy stationery?
What reading fuels your writing?
What kind of writing do you admire but hate to read?
Why do you write?
Do you think you are a writer?
When did you define yourself as a writer?
How would your readers describe you?
What one piece of writing that you have written, or would like to write, would you like to be remembered by?
What has been the best writing lesson: that you have learned; that you were in; that you taught?
What is the kind of writing you most like to teach?

Invent your own list of questions. Divide into pairs and interview each other, using as many or as few questions as you wish. Ask the questions in any order. You may find that one question is enough. The next step is to write at length. Write about your own experience or about the person you have interviewed.

Writing metaphors

For this, you need a collection of disparate objects. Don't overthink this and don't choose objects that you think will match the task. Each writer chooses an object. The task is to write using the object as a metaphor for writing. Try and avoid objects that immediately lend themselves to the task, for example, a string of beads is an image already overused to describe writing. Although there are objects that suggest themselves more readily as metaphors for writing, it pays dividends to choose something that at first glance seems unlikely. Our collections include: various cheap plastic toys, including a pair of wind-up teeth and a flick-a-chicken (don't ask); a champagne cork; a half-used Paracetamol packet; birthday cake candles; swimming goggles; . . .

> It occurs to me that writing is, in many ways, like a Six Way Party Moustache.
> The striking similarity suggested itself to me the moment I read: 'Shape It Any Way You Like' on the knowingly retro packaging of the whimsical whiskers. Could there be any more apt metaphor for the invitation writing extends to the individual to fashion language into whatever fanciful forms their imagination can devise than that of the encouragement – nay challenge – to 'shape' the moustache 'any way you like'? This advertiser's enticement (incitement?) seems to me to embody precisely the alluringly unfettered possibilities of expression that the act of writing offers . . .
>
> (Secondary teacher)

. . . and so on. This activity allows for playfulness and that pushing of the thought process that writing sometimes demands.

References

Andrews, R. & Smith, A. (2011) *Developing Writers: Teaching and Learning in the Digital Age.* Maidenhead: Open University Press.

Cremin, T. & Baker, S. (2014) 'Exploring the discursively constructed identities of a teacher-writer teaching writing.' In *English Teaching Practice and Critique*, 13(3), 30–55.

Krementz, J. (1996) *The Writer's Desk.* New York: Random House.

Morley, D. (2007) *The Cambridge Introduction to Creative Writing.* Cambridge: CUP.

Wenger, E. (1998) *Communities of Practice.* Cambridge: CUP.

Chapter 12

Our own writing
What do teachers write?

This chapter celebrates the writing of teachers who are already members of NWP (UK) groups. Teachers' writing is threaded throughout this book and demonstrates something of what we believe writing can do. Teachers write in order to think, to engage with memory and their inner selves, to record important events, to develop an argument, to create stories and shape poetry. They write lists, journals, research papers, novels. They do not clamp writing into any one particular box. What you should find here is a sense of the variety and energy that emerges from teachers' writing groups, a meditation on writing and a series of writing prompts that you might wish to use yourself.

Writing in the museum

I wrote [this] in response to time at the Museum of London. I was taken by the poetry of the signage before I could even enter the room. It provoked me to consider words/writing and communication.

Gifts from the River Thames
'Artery, boundary, larder, sacred stream'

Artery, boundary, larder, sacred stream,
that's all the good words taken then.
They've already said
what I wanted to say.

So it's silence
Or
Letting each word
Reverberate
In a new way
Just for you and me.

Our arteries are pumping blood,
See
We're still alive,

Boundary is harder-
Look
Where do you end
And I begin?

Ah, the larder,
Our favourite room
The first place the boys still go
When they come home.

And the sacred stream
Much, much harder,
Rivers we plunged through
Rocky Mountain fed, Ausengate iced,
Lake District rain swollen
Or
Smaller streams
of river walking
Dam building
Splash jumping
Children,
The River Stour
Home.

A collection

This writing came from a session based on what we had in our pockets/a collection of some-thing. In the session I chose to use the items that happened to be in my pocket, but I also took with me a small blue marble. This marble came from a huge collection I'd gathered over the years with my granddad, and represented the much larger collection. I wrote an entirely different piece at the time, but my thoughts kept returning to the marble. As I was walk-ing home from the session, I was fiddling with the marble and staring up at the stars, when I heard an angry cyclist yelling, 'Oh for god's sake, what do you want?' at a car which had veered a little too close. And the idea took off.

As he laid on his back gazing up into the vastness of the universe he became pain-fully aware that he was just a man, on a tiny blue marble spinning around a rather little sun at the edge of one of the smaller known galaxies.

'Oh great lord,' he cried in his despair, 'what is the point of it all? Oh, please tell me. Answer me, won't you?' He sighed as the only response was the faint echo of his own voice. He stood, giving up.

'What?' A voice came, seemingly from within his own head.

'Hello? Who's there?'

'Who do you think is here? The one you've been wailing at for the last five minutes. I'm your god, aren't I?'

'Oh really?' He smirked, 'prove it then.'

'Seriously? You moan and whine that you want me to talk to you, I do it, and now you want proof? Forget it!'

'No, no. I'm sorry.' The man fell to his knees, 'Please stay.'

'Oh do get up, you idiot. Look, I don't have all day. What do you want?'

'I want to know why?'

'Why what?'

'Well, I want to know what our purpose is. Why're we here? Why did you create us?'

'Ah, you're one of those.' Sighed the god. 'I see. I'll tell you the same thing I told Wilde, and the same thing I told Marx: Look at your planet. You have air, you have food, you have water. More importantly, you have love, beauty and fun. For pity's sake – you live on the only world with waterparks. The *only* one. There are over 500 billion planets in your galaxy alone, and yours is the only one where you can throw yourself down a *wet* slide for the sake of fun. And is it enough? No! You need some higher calling. Some purpose. Oh but that purpose can't just be *to have fun*. No, that's not good enough. It has to be serious. It has to be depressing. Well you know what? I've had enough. Screw you.'

And with that, a tiny blue marble, spinning around a little sun at the edge of one of the smaller known galaxies winked out of existence.

A personal choice

I wrote this poem in the days after my ex-husband moved out. The worst of the pain was over and no drama remained. I felt utterly drained, so I tried to give the poem a stillness to reflect this. His absence was made conspicuous by the fact that after years of listening to him playing the piano in our house, I could still hear the music now that he had gone. A sort of earworm, I suppose.

Writing the poem helped me dispel an un-ease with my surroundings caused by his conspicuous absence. Sharing the poem and receiving feedback took away some of the aloneness of it all.

Reading it now, gives me a visceral memory of something past. I'm glad I wrote and shared it. I see this piece of writing as forming part of my recovery from the breakdown of such an important relationship.

The Absence

In the house without the man, a sound ghost shadows me,
Close harmony escapes from the cupboard which holds the fuse-box,
Clair de Lune when I open the refrigerator,
Wide spaced chords as I climb the stairs.

Kind of Blue,

Some Day My Prince will Come.

Museum of London

1. *Arnicated Corn Cream: The name, the box, the packaging, the concept – everything fascinated me.*
2. *1878, the first escalator was installed in the UK in Harrods. This fact gave me mixed feelings – ones of fear and interest as this fact has such a personal significance for me because I have a phobia of escalators. I am petrified of going down them. A very difficult phobia if you live in London and want to get around by travelling on the tube, but I plan my journey around avoiding them and people are really surprised when they learn this because I manage to arrive everywhere I need to be.*
3. *A brief biography of Kamal Chunchie who was born in 1886 and died 1953. He worked in race relations, was a social justice champion in the East End of London and founded The Coloured Men's Institute. It captivated me that many of the struggles that he worked for over 100 years ago, some people are still working for today.*

I was clasping the hand of my mother and hop-skipping to try and catch up with her. My arms were being disagreeably pulled in opposite directions, for behind me was my neighbour, Jack, who was clinging onto my hand for dear life. Jack was a sickly boy – pale and thin with wisps of black hair and sunken watery eyes. . . .

Jack's hand was clammy and kept slipping out of mine. Eventually I grabbed his wrist, my shoulder clicked agonisingly but at least I wouldn't lose him.

Ammi, my mother, strode purposefully through the crowd of opulent dresses and exquisite hats, dressed in her best yellow and turquoise saree. She was a woman on a mission: smelling salts and arnicated corn cream, both of which she had been reliably informed were available in Harrods (the most superior quality that is, and for Ammi, only the best would do). I cringed as people moved out of her way, expressions ranging from curiosity and wonderment to downright revulsion and loathing. But Ammi was a strong woman and she didn't care. She was a matriarch and she ran her life, her family and everything associated with the two things as she wished, like clockwork.

We whizzed past exotic spices, enticing sweet jars and elegant stationery, up the stairs and into the chemist. After Ammi had approved of and purchased the required items, we turned around to make our way out of the store. Ammi, now more relaxed that she had completed her errand, was chatting to us and asking if we would like cake and tea. Suddenly, she stopped dead and went pale. This was the first time I had seen mother lost for words in this way. There in front of us, was an unusual sight: moving stairs. We watched amazed. Wooden steps carried people up. It was magic as person after person arrived, looking pleased, excited and slightly relieved. Each one seemed to "pop" over at a certain point and Jack and I stood watching and guessing whether a man, woman or child would appear next. Ammi, however, looked panicked and petrified. She was breathing rapidly, a cold sweat on her forehead as her eyes darted up and down. She murmured to herself "Oh Lord! What magic is this? What death trap? What work of the devil? These are the Final Times, Kamal, I tell you, the Final Times! The death of mankind! We now no longer even have to walk up the stairs . . ."

I watched Ammi bemused until I noticed two things. Firstly, Jack looked like he was about to collapse so I put my arm around him to support him and secondly, the family that were looking at us with undisguised disgust and contempt. At first, I thought it was just me and I pushed back my chest with pride. I was not ashamed of who I was- not my skin colour, not my language, not my spicy, aromatic food and certainly not my dignified Ammi with her brightly coloured saree.

But then I realised with alarm that Jack with his patched trousers and threadbare coat was also included in that stare.

'THOSE types shouldn't be allowed to mix with US . . .'

I very much enjoyed writing this piece . . . I felt that I could almost see it in my eyes . . . It reminded me also of my own mum who also doesn't care that she "looks" different and just goes about her own business every day.

A list

This poem is from a favourite writing session . . . It is a list poem inspired by Peter Stillman's poem about his past cars. I wrote about events on 'nights out' with friends, in roughly chronological order, from my teenage years through university to the present. The title is a homage to a Regina Spektor song "That Time" which I love and has a similar theme and structure.

I think the list form is very accessible (I enjoy structured ideas) and appeals to the sentimental side of me (I love recording and writing about things that have happened in my life). I actually think it's also really accessible for the age range I work with, which is nursery. They can come up with ideas and put them together in this form without having to have a lot of prior knowledge about how poetry is structured. So I guess my next steps are to do this more!

Hey Remember That Time . . .

The time I wore a grown up sweater to avoid suspicion.
The time someone stole a Robert Hale Homes for Sale sign.
The time I spent all the money in my purse.
The time I listened to Braille with my eyes closed.
The time Nips wore his trainers at midnight.
The time Jade ripped off her sleeves.
The time I shook my tail feather.
The time everyone got lost.
The time I dressed as a sunflower.

The time we saw a clown.
The time Kyle cut his chin open.
The time we played Bananagrams.
The time I nearly got crushed by a fridge.
The time we sung Hakuna Matata.
The time we stayed in and read Chat instead.

Apples

'Apples heaped on market barrows . . .' I read aloud to my daughter nightly. Every time, I smell the narrow passage down the side of Grandma's house, heaped with summer's apples in buckets each September; the smell of Autumn coming, and Sundays, and going back to school.

I'm standing on a wooden ladder leaned against the trunk, twisting apples which yield easily into my hand and throwing them to my sister below. Proper apples, with leafy stalks, caterpillar and maggot holes out of which things could come creeping.

Grandma's garden was full of frights: the unearthed spider carrying its millions of eggs, huge bees in the foxgloves, Grandpa in his shed. But also the hedgehog we would leave milk for, the blue tits zooming out of the hole of the nesting box each spring, and the blackbirds splashing in the stone birdbath beneath the kitchen window.

A summer garden party for the French cousins. Crawling through the green light of the poly-tunnel, climbing the apple tree, jumping over the bamboo stick and peg high jump. I twisted my ankle and sat in the blue kitchen with my foot in the washing up bowl.

The apple smell would reach its peak and it was time to make the Christmas cake. Sifting flour to make it snow. Stirring the thick, stodgy mix, sniffing the nutmeg and cinnamon. There were frights in the larder, especially in the jam jars. 'Just scrape it off, it's fine underneath.'

The cake sat centre stage in its ruff. The perfect cousins wore ties, dad went to watch telly on his own upstairs. Uncle Jim's mum sat chain smoking in the corner. Great-Grandma, regal and cold, in turban and diamonds, watched through hooded eyes. Every year the cake, long after they were all gone – Great-Grandma, dad, Jim – and the world had been rocked to its core by a French cousin bringing her girlfriend for Christmas.

We'd follow Grandma to and from the kitchen, seeing her busy. She'd warn us to stay well away from the microwave in case it cooked our brains inside out. This was the kitchen of kippers and croissants on a weekend morning, bones boiling in saucepans, Delia, pie pastry, and her small can of Carlsberg fizzing on the side while Sunday lunch was cooked to the sounds of Desert Island Discs.

Nothing has ever been better than a poached egg on toast for tea in that blue kitchen, or coming down the passage to the back door, smelling those apples heavy with the last of summer.

*This piece uses a stimulus from Goldberg's **Old Friend From Far Away** (2007). Before I knew where I was going to go, I began a sensory ramble back in time, starting with an apple. This is writing purely to please myself. The first thing I can see about it is that it wouldn't pass muster at GCSE – fragment sentences! Tense shifting! I'm also not sure about the detour of the Christmas paragraph. The feeling I had when writing was the same I had writing as a child. I was there – walking up the passageway, knowing exactly what I'd see next. I knew the texture of the door handle. Dead people were alive. I was six, ten, fourteen. Writing the place and people took me straight back to them in a way that I couldn't achieve if I was to sit and try to conjure them. The apple smell was tantalisingly close, at the edges of my nose.*

Who or what was that writing for? I read it to my sister, because it evokes associated memories only we share. Why 'weekend breakfasts' at Grandma's? We lived there during the divorce. Why was that kitchen 'safe'? Nobody was violent there. Why has 'nothing ever been better'? Life had a serene order there we hadn't previously experienced – the stolidity of my grandparents' lives was utterly exotic to us. I'd never have written about these things as a child, for a teacher to read, because family circumstances were a shameful secret and my parents needed to be protected- writing was an escape from all that, took me far away.

Writing in class

This is my favourite piece of 2014, and something I would love to develop into something more. We were writing suspense, and to be honest I just got carried away whilst the children were busy writing. There's a fervent atmosphere in the classroom when 25 children and the teacher are writing away. Perhaps I need to get teaching assistants involved in future as well.

The real challenge here was to remain as ambiguous as possible. Normally I'm a 'skip to the end' writer, but this is far more the effort I'd have to go to if I ever were to write my own novel.

Leaves rustled. An owl hooted eerily. It was dark. The creature liked the dark. It was safe in the dark. The creature's many legs carried it quickly across the ground, though the slightest noise caused the creature to stop. Maybe it wasn't so safe in the dark after all.

Up ahead was the tree. The ancient, withered tree. The only tree around that was leafless all year round. Was it dead? Lightning struck the sky, illuminating the dark for the briefest of moments. In those moments, the tree looked more dangerous than ever. Its silhouette loomed over the creature.

Once the brightness had passed, the creature felt safe once more. Time to move again. The closest word in our language to describe the creature's movements would be 'scuttling,' but this doesn't quite match. The multiple legs worked in unison as the creature moved from shadow to shadow. Thunder broke the rustling with an echoing boom. Pairs of feet froze. As the thunder resided, those pairs thawed and picked up the pace. The tree still seemed too far away. Still time to escape. Even the dangerous, vicious looking tree was a better place to be than outside.

Overhead, the residual crackle of the lightning hung in the air, just long enough to make the tiniest of hairs tingle. Nights like these weren't common, but were becoming ever more so. In spite of this, there was still something of the lightning to be savoured, like the nights of old where the finest of foods were readily available. Those days were no more. Times had most definitely changed.

'Scuttling' once more, the creature edged closer to the tree. About three, maybe four minutes now. A few minutes to avoid the ever-present danger in the air. The creature moved from shadow to shadow, eyes darted like dragonflies, leaving nowhere uncovered.

The vivid turquoise lightning crackled across the sky again. Tightly woven scales shimmered across its back. In the glowing light, the exact colour and nature of them were unclear. It had been a long time since one of these had been seen in this part of the world.

From the boughs of the tree, which, despite its appearance, was physically no more special than those around it, an altogether more upright being, with far fewer legs, stood guard. As had been the way for centuries, the tree needed protection. A certain significance and history demanded it, though the origins had long been forgotten.

Hiraeth and Hinterlands

I nearly didn't come today. I signed up to this writing group meeting months ago, before the Welsh rugby team started their winning streak; before I realised that this afternoon would see them trying to win the Grand Slam in Cardiff; before I felt the tug of my old home pulling me towards a pub:

> Mae hen wlad fy nhadau yn annwyl i mi . . .
> *The old land of my fathers is dear to me . . .*

My dear old father wanted me to have roots, to know that my personal history is grounded in the coal fields of Merthyr Tydfil and the steel works of Port Talbot. My warm, oh-so-Welsh mother wanted me to understand the language of my ancestors and the poetry of my land:

> Gwlad beirdd a chantorion, enwogion o fri . . .
> *Land of bards and singers, honoured and free . . .*

Both parents also wished me to fly: 'give the children roots and wings', they said.

I left Wales twenty five years ago and flew. For a decade, I travelled light in North America, Europe and Southern Africa. I rejected what I came to see as petty, national pride and stopped watching the boys in red. I developed deep, cross-continental friendships. 'She's a child of the world now', mam would say.

But while wandering, I always knew the word 'hiraeth'. Hard to translate into English, it means a longing, or yearning, for the Wales of the past. I think of it as a visceral attachment to an inevitably ephemeral landscape and culture. Despite my meanderings, the old land of my fathers was lodged in my soul, and when I had children of my own, I settled in London and started watching rugby again. From time to time I experience a strong sense of hiraeth, which is almost overwhelming when Wales play in the Six Nations. So I nearly didn't come today.

On arrival, slightly distracted, I greet with a hug colleagues that I have been writing with for years now. It is good to see these people, but I am fidgety as I feel my phone with my fingers.

We begin, as we always do, by penning something ourselves. When we split into small groups to share what we have written, I first listen to Morlette read an emotional and evocative description of a vivid scene from her youth in South Africa. Her words are so full of feeling and her memories so raw that as she reads, she weeps and as I listen, captivated, a tear runs down my face. I recognise her sense of hiraeth and when our group talks about her beautifully written recollection, we connect:

Only connect the prose and the passion, and both will be exalted. . .

That was it! That was why I came then. That was the card that trumped the rugby. I came to connect with an English teaching community which has articulated – down the generations – the importance of personal growth through writing. Sometimes, that notion, *that hinterland*, has been at risk of getting lost in stock cupboards stuffed with ring binders which attempt to 'inventorise' writing. Sometimes, our collective sense of self has suffocated under a mass of directives on assessment, designed to ensure that literacy is functional (but with the unintended consequence of ridding any trace of individual experience from the English classroom). As the philosopher MacMurray so brilliantly articulated, the functional life is *for* the personal life and not the other way around. I came to communicate with a committed collective of people who want to rescue English from a narrow instrumentalism and build a powerful, national movement of writers' groups which reasserts the importance of the personal, with the functional as the important servant but never the master.

As I walk to the nearest tube station, I pass a pub in which there is standing room only and all eyes are on the big screen. I jostle my way into the heart of the crowd and see that Wales are still playing France. They have a narrow lead with ten minutes to go. I stand transfixed, on tiptoes, biting my bottom lip. When the final whistle blows, I wander back out into the light smiling and determined.

Chapter 13

Reflecting on teaching

> [The writing group] . . . has awakened my love of attempting to write about my own teaching experiences, which has lead me to become more reflective, and experimental with my ideas in the classroom.
>
> (Early Years teacher)

Teachers' writing groups embody an approach to professional development based on a philosophy that recognises the importance of teacher knowledge, expertise and leadership. It is an approach that values the experience that teachers bring to and from their classrooms and assumes that professional growth is best served when teachers share their knowledge and expertise with each other as peers. Teachers' writing groups are built on a belief that teachers are key agents for transforming how writing is perceived, practised and assessed in their classrooms. In sharing the narratives of their classrooms teachers take the opportunity to redirect and reshape their practice.

A growing number of teachers in groups choose to research their teaching of writing as part of accredited study or for their own pleasure and professional development. Groups spend time discussing teaching with a varying degree of formality. Such discussion generally arises either in response to the experience of writing and sharing writing or in response to evidence brought from classrooms. The Buckinghamshire TAW project and the UEA Writing Teachers have reflected on teaching, more formally, as part of gathering evidence. The Buckinghamshire group contributed regularly to a VLE, writing directly to others engaged in the same project, sharing experiences and seeking advice. In preparing this book, we have drawn on this evidence and have asked teachers in all groups to contribute by responding to a brief set of prompts.

Many writing teachers keep journals. Some keep a separate reflective teaching journal and others find that the reflections on teaching mingle with writing for their own purposes.

Keeping a reflective teaching journal

Capturing what happens in our writing classrooms and having time, sometimes, to reflect on that is not only interesting for the writer, but could contribute to our growing, collective understanding of the nature of teaching writing at the beginning of the twenty-first century. If you decide to keep a teaching journal, Gilly Bolton's book, *Reflective Practice* (2014), is full of insight and practical approaches to using writing as reflection.

What you make of a teaching journal depends very much on you and your particular circumstances. As with any other writing, it can be almost anything you want it to be. In the first place it can be a notebook in which you record things that are interesting to you that happen during the teaching day. You may write, but may also wish to use a camera or iPad and relevant software in order to keep a multimodal record. You might begin simply by recording anything that catches your interest: a snippet of conversation, the reaction of a group to a task, an observation of a child writing or a record of one's plans and intentions and what actually happened. You are likely to notice patterns that point to the questions that are most important to you. Once you have those questions, the journal may have greater focus. A journal is a way of holding on to the constantly moving events of the classroom and then trying to make some sense of them. It allows us to pause and then to explore the beliefs and theories which arise from and inform our actions in the classroom.

Try to keep a daily journal. The reality is that it may be more sporadic. Get into the habit of capturing at least one small thing each day. Try writing it at the end of the day, at the end of a particular lesson or even during it. It can be useful to jot down thoughts or to record things when talking with an individual or group – in which case it may become part of the conversation and the learning process. Once you have kept a journal for any length of time, you may begin to see patterns and this may lead you to write at greater length. Try beginning with the story – write down what happened – and then let the pen take you. Thoughts and questions seem to arise quite easily – and sometimes unexpectedly. Think about using the raw material of the day-to-day journal to explore the thoughts and beliefs which lie behind the actions. Tease out what the observations tell you. Start with a single event or perhaps several that link, and write freely, not worrying about formal writing, but rather writing as things come to mind, not always completing the sentence; write lists; ask questions.

What are you able to learn about the ways in which writing for yourself is reflected in your teaching?

> The fact that I am now making time every few days to put thoughts down on the page is exciting. I am more in tune with the challenges that face our students when the time to write begins. I have been able to use some of my own experience to help guide young writers along, to encourage them to take risks, to make them feel a sense of pride in their own expression.
>
> (Secondary teacher)

One challenge for a teachers' writing group is how to capture the ways in which being a part of writing teachers is reflected in their teaching. The impact of writing together may appear during planning and organisation and is very likely to be present in decisions made while teaching. One particular challenge in terms of measuring the impact is that almost as soon as a teacher has joined a group their teaching changes so that it feels to them as if that is how it has always been. We have found that writing about teaching often goes hand in hand with writing about our writing. Earliest reactions to working with NWP groups relate to writers' feelings about themselves as writers and their different empathy towards those they teach. It is not unusual for teachers to wonder how they have come to be teaching writing in the ways they have become accustomed to.

> Has it changed the way I teach? Absolutely. Now, when I demonstrate writing in class, I am less inclined to magic up a McExtract which captures a pre-specified objective and more inclined to write whatever the students are writing. I try not to tell students to be quiet and work while I patrol the rows; I make the effort to take up my pen with pleasure. My starting point is less often a text type or a technique and more often a stimulus which I think my pupils will enjoy. As a result, the students seem less resentful and more respectful of the writing process. When we share our work, which is now more likely than before to reveal shards of ourselves, I encourage students to listen carefully and to comment. I struggle to give levels and to standardise, but that does not mean that I do not assess. At the end of the lesson, I ask everyone to reflect on what they have learned. I reflect too because at the beginning of the class, I could not have anticipated what would emerge.
>
> (Secondary teacher)

Writing alongside

Writing alongside children is perhaps the most significant change that teachers identify. It is a suggestion rather than an expectation but one that teachers choose. They continue because of the impact it has on young writers. The changes begin with teachers' own experience of writing.

> This excitement and greater depth of understanding has led me to become far more involved in my own writing lessons. I have the confidence to share pieces I have written and to ask for and accept the comments and criticisms of the children. I love sharing the task or activity I have set and writing alongside them. Previously this would have been worrying, now it is fun.
>
> (Secondary teacher)

Many teachers initially feel unsure about this. However, teachers from long-standing groups would say that this has become a crucial element of their practice. The truth is that students love the fact that you write and are generous in their praise. They like it when you get it just right and they are reassured when it doesn't always go right for you. You may not always have time to write all the time because you will want to teach in different ways at different times. However, writing with students and sharing some of what you write has an impact. You become a writer alongside them.

If I then think about all I have said about myself as a writer and put this into the context of a child sitting in my class, I immediately find that my understanding has increased. I no longer feel that children should necessarily share. If I felt inadequate in a very safe situation, how must some of my year 5s feel? I now have greater respect for their writing and their privacy, although I still have a long way to go to get some of my colleagues to understand this. I can (and do) of course model being brave and this has had tangible effects on the writing of some groups. One child, when I posed the question: Why is it helpful if I write with you and then share? said that he felt it showed we were all in it together and he loved it when I read out something that I decided wasn't terribly good and should be altered!

(Primary teacher)

It seems that the writing group creates a context where teachers have a chance to cultivate the 'other self' that Donald Murray advocates (1982). Perhaps teachers develop not only the voice of their inner writing partner, but the voice they need as teachers of young writers. To write alongside those we teach is a paradigm shift for most teachers, especially in the current climate, yet teachers quickly find it has an impact on children's motivation and confidence. When we write alongside our pupils we make ourselves vulnerable. We would argue that this is a position of strength for a teacher, but only if the vulnerability is rooted in understanding and in the mutual support a writing group can provide. Writing alongside children is not an end in itself but part of the more inclusive principle behind the creation of a community of learners. Teachers do not simply write at the same time as their students but are willing to share their writing, their difficulties and the way they approach writing.

Tomorrow I have planned a lesson where I show my chain of thoughts and how I adapted and improved it. Hopefully they can then do the same. I hope to share my experiences that improving and editing work can be fun and satisfying.

(Secondary teacher)

A strong, trusted writing community lays the foundations for growth. Teachers learn to love writing and communicate their pleasure to those they teach and are able to take risks and share problems with them also.

A context for writing

Through working together, the Buckinghamshire group became preoccupied with the context for writing, understanding the difficulties 'and perceived difficulties' that children might face. They noted the value of having an audience and how, in the first instance, that audience can be the group with whom you write. Empathy with young writers has led teachers to reconsider the tasks they set, how they set them, and their expectations of their written work. They come to understand the individuality of writing and its unevenness. How it can become vital in developing thought in all curriculum subjects (D'Arcy 1989) and on personal growth. How writing can be frothy and playful. How hitting the right spot can be a joyful thing, An extract from this teacher's list of ways in which joining the project has had an impact on her teaching summarises the group's preoccupations present at the beginning of the project and clarified through practice:

- I give the children far more choice, that may be in title, subject matter, presentation, genre. Choice seems to give the children a firmer feeling of ownership of what they are writing.
- The children have writing journals and a large amount of freedom in using them. I give time during the week . . . and the children choose whether or not they wish to share.
- I am far more attuned to difficulties that children may have with writing . . . or sometimes perceive they have.
- I am far more aware of the fact that . . . writing can be tricksy. It is personal and there can be a myriad of reasons as to why a child would perform on one day and not the next or in one activity and not others.
- A clearer grasp that writing can be and is important and relevant in every subject. Cross-curricular approaches can make writing more real and relevant to children and of course an audience . . . even writing fairy tales for reception . . . makes the writing task more purposeful and important . . . and fun. Important word fun!
- TAW and the experiences attached to it have given me a heightened awareness in the classroom of the holistic possibilities surrounding writing. I now have children who write diaries, who are on their 3rd or 4th writing journal and who list writing as a major out of school interest!

(Primary teacher)

This teacher extended the sense of community from a single classroom, across the school:

Using student writing examples across year groups has also been very interesting. When I use work from upper years as exemplar material for younger students, the message they seem to come away with is 'Wow, I can do that!' which is very empowering and gives them a sense of worth. When I show the work of younger years to older groups, they tend to be even more amazed. The creativity and depth, the strength of ideas is something that they appreciate. Research shows that creativity can tend to dwindle as students pass through the school system . . . hopefully regular exercise of the writing muscles will do something to resolve this.

(Secondary teacher)

Once teachers have been working from the strength of a community of writers, and have applied some of those principles to their teaching, they begin to note the impact that it is having on individuals and groups of children:

Over the past few months I have seen some unlikely students have some incredible successes. The 'popular girls' who intimidated some in the class were producing works of depth, sensitivity, and confidently revealing some of their inner thoughts and feelings. The 'sporty boys' who have begun to see their imagination, their games with language, the clarity and quality of their expression as something to brag about, something to value and to respect. The 'quiet ones' who have found a voice and the confidence to read out a piece of work that would have been lost to silence otherwise, I have seen the look in their faces when others in the class speak up to praise them.

(Secondary teacher)

Teachers note their willingness 'to try out different ideas and see where the writing process takes us'. The impact that their teaching was having on 'boy-heavy' groups, ('The end of year results. . . . have been very much better than expected and for boys is well above the National Average.'), on children with special educational needs (SEN) and those who had formerly seemed utterly resistant, who would 'come into the class-room and begin complaining before they reached their seats: "It's cold!", "Not that again!", "Can I move seats?"' was notable.

Teaching writing in the classroom has become more and more about celebration of voice and affirmation rather than about results. It's a fantastic side effect that results are sustained or improved by celebration. Last week, . . . a Year 9 writer, chose to join the creative writing workshop when he normally would have chosen House Sports. This is a remarkable achievement! I have been astonished and touched and filled with gratitude for my job when working with young writers in a whole new way since learning from TAW.

(Secondary teacher)

Teachers and children feel empowered by the opportunity to write freely and to discuss their writing. However, in the present context, the 'creative writing' class may well be separate from other forms of school writing or may appear only in writing clubs. Teachers who are growing to understand the strength of freer writing, also, properly, have questions.

We are generally agreed that it is easy to forget the complexity of the process of 'being' a writer, and subjecting ourselves to the same kind of pressures and per-haps vulnerability that we invite our students to is important. Preoccupations are with the building blocks. We are great at having good ideas to stimulate writing (our own and in the classroom) but it is the next steps phase that is more difficult.

(Secondary teacher)

The first step, for both teachers and children, is to gain the confidence and the enjoy-ment in writing that will provide the foundations for growth. Terry Locke (2014) sug-gests a highly principled 'program of professional reclamation' that depends on the kind of networks that writing groups create. A next step is to explore some of the questions that teachers' writing group do, and must, engage with.

- What do we understand by writing development?
- What kinds of assessment might best serve young writers?
- What might be the qualities of good writing at different stages?
- What are the understandings, knowledge and skills that will best equip young writers at different stages of their lives?
- What knowledge, understandings and skill does the teacher need in order to best develop writers?
- What does classroom practice look like where young writers learn best?

A teaching journal

What you choose to record will depend on your interests and situation. These questions and ideas may help you to focus your thought – or, at least, to decide what you don't want to do:

What were your thoughts in planning an activity? Did it turn out as you expected? How did the children's responses differ from your expectations?

How well were you able to respond to what happened?

What seemed to help things along? What seemed to get in the way?

Is your idea of a fruitful lesson different from that of those you are teaching?

How are children negotiating responses and meanings?

Is there resistance? Celebration? Are children able to take from you and make it their own? Make it something new?

What are the surprises?

What are the comforts/the discomforts?

What is rippling the surface?

What seems to be going on?

Good moments . . . what are they? Are you able to repeat them . . . sometimes?

Experiments, hunches, immediate responses . . . what happened? How did it work out?

Anything that has made you (or children) excited, worried, angry, intrigued? What? Why?

So what?

Where did it come from?

Where might it go?

What if . . .? How . . .? Why . . .? What . . .? If only . . .

Lists:

- of likes
- of questions
- of things that you think have influenced you

- of things that you don't know and would like to know
- of answers
- of books you are reading
- of ideas that intrigue you

Maps and drawings:

- of your thoughts
- of a lesson
- of something that you are reading but is hard to understand
- of your feelings through a lesson or series of lessons

Unsent letters; letters that you write but do not send . . . or maybe you will:

- to a child in your class
- to someone who has taught you
- to someone who is teaching you now
- to the author of a book or article which has caught your attention
- to a fellow teacher

A description
A description with footnotes
A dialogue with a teacher, a colleague, a child, a writer, with your alter ego.
A portrait of a child in your class
A response to a piece of writing from: a child; a friend or colleague; a published author; yourself.

References

Bolton, G. (2014) *Reflective Practice: Writing and Professional Development.* 4th Ed. London: Sage.

D'Arcy, P. (1989) *Making Sense, Shaping Meaning: Writing in the Context of a Capacity-based Approach to Learning.* Ports, NH: Boynton/Cook.

Locke, T. (2014) *Developing Writing Teachers: Practical Ways for Teacher-writers to Transform their Classroom Practice.* London & New York: Routledge.

Murray, D.M. (1982) 'The Listening Eye.' In *Learning by Teaching.* Montclair, NJ: Boynton/Cook.

Chapter 14

Establishing children's writing groups

Writing clubs can provide the opportunity for extra support or for longer writing experiments in a non-judgmental space. Some children surprise themselves and their teachers with what they are able to write with a different, mixed-age, peer group. When writing is valued for its authenticity of voice and freshness of perspective, writers gain the insight and confidence in how to make progress in other ways.

The following paragraphs describe three different teachers' experiences of writing clubs. All three teachers were members of Buckinghamshire's TAW project. They each adapted TAW approaches and wrote alongside their children/students.

Lynda, set up a lunchtime writing club, 'Buzzwords', in her primary school. She began with Year 6 children and, after a while, opened the club to children from across KS2. Children were given writing notebooks and encouraged to 'loosen their writing muscles' with a range of word hunts, lists and short writing exercises. She found oral anecdotes and memories powerful ways of engaging less confident writers. She always read aloud a piece of writing to broaden the children's vocabulary, ideas, and structures and to increase their literary knowledge. A collection of simple writing prompts also proved effectively flexible resources – pictures, maps, word collections, opening lines and headlines. Children were happy to find their own materials and spaces, under desks as well as at them, and to write for twenty minutes. Lynda established an atmosphere of respectful attention so children who wanted to would read out their work. They were always keen to know their peers' responses and became fond of each other's distinctive humour.

Lynda identifies children's increased ease with writing as the greatest success. This was especially the case for children with learning difficulties who had previously under-achieved because of low self-esteem, and for abler writers who had been hampered by the limitations of prescribed or over-structured writing tasks.

Patrick Donoghue, ran a KS3 writing club to instil a sense of pride in his students' accomplishments and give them confidence and willingness to take on any task that was put in front of them. He launched the club on National Poetry Day 2011 and chose a sporting theme. He engaged students by projecting sporting words, music and images. He used provocative quotations from writers and sports stars. The students were invited to live the sporting dream and write their own 'sporting boast'. Over the weeks that followed, the students played 'poetry tag', spring-boarding from each other's words and ideas. They conducted a 'scavenger hunt' around the playing fields and sports halls. They read Simon Armitage's 'The Catch', watching slow-motion film of sporting movements in order to charge their writing with detail and emotion. They used computer programs to create interactive stories with different pathways, using hyperlinks.

Some of the students commented:

> In September I was really, really nervous about my writing. I never used to like writing stories but now I love writing them and I write at least one a week.

> We get choice and I like it . . . fun ways, short tasks, computers . . .

> We can get help with our writing cos there's less of us

After a few weeks of the writing club, Patrick reflected on the changes in attitude and achievement in writing for different groups of students:

> Some were able to confidently express themselves with a great deal of sensitivity and sophistication. Some of the sportier students are seeing language as a game – and their skill of expressing themselves clearly and creatively as something to brag about. And . . . the more quiet students who found a voice in the English classroom and the look on their faces when some of their fellow students are praising them for what they've written is really, really memorable.

Emma, has set up writing clubs in three different schools. She did so to extend the schools' curriculum offer – a chance to take writing beyond the scope of lessons. In 2013, when she wanted to offer students the chance to follow AQA's Creative Writing AS and A levels, a club was the only option: the timetable was too crowded; the specification was unproven; the numbers were too few. Writers emerged from all ages and curriculum areas – sometimes to gain a qualification; sometimes, at their peers' invitation, just to come and enjoy writing. The space and 'permission' to write personally and imaginatively, to experiment with new structures and devices, helped those secret writers who harboured ambitions and just needed a little extra support to explore reading and writing further and make their own discoveries.

One of the greatest successes was students' increased ability to be each other's teachers. In one school the sixth formers led sessions for others on a whole-school writing day. Confidence gained in the club also led to students' higher attainment in English Literature and an interest in studying Creative Writing at undergraduate level.

How can teachers go about setting up a writing club/group?

On your own:

- Start writing today.
- Fix a regular time when you can sit comfortably and quietly, and aim to write for at least 20 minutes. Sometimes this will be easy and you'll write longer; sometimes

this will be hard and you'll seize up. But you need to gain confidence to write even when you're not feeling like it. So writing 'rubbish' and lists, recounts and observations can help to get the flow going. Try out the ideas you plan to use with the writing group. Your experience is invaluable if you're going to help others gain confidence. Time and date your journal entries and count up how many words you've written in the time you had. Then you'll know what's possible. Once you've done this for a week or so, you'll be ready to start. You don't have to share any of this by reading it out to your club or class, but it really helps to write alongside pupils, using the same prompts, and to be prepared to show, share and discuss some of the evidence. Your example will be very powerful in communicating your belief to pupils, and they will benefit from listening to your writing aims, processes and products – but you judge what you want to read out and when.

With the children:

- **Sound out your individuals and classes diplomatically.** Identify your keen writers. Discuss the idea with them. Establish a convenient lunchtime or after-school time, so that you can meet once a week for at least half a term before you review or change anything. Engage your enthusiasts by word of mouth, and advertise.
  In a primary school assembly with about 300 children, one teacher announced the start of her Year 5 and 6 writing club with these words: 'I will be doing this in Mrs X's classroom at lunchtime. If you would like to come along, we're going to be writing things that we want to write and, you know, it's for fun, basically.' Seventeen children came to the first session and twenty-five to the second. The club is still running after two years.
- **Aim for it to be a fun and stress-free time** with a range of quick writing games and short challenges. Meet in a quiet place. Give each writer a notebook and pen, or encourage them to buy a nice one. Establish some ground rules about privacy, experimentation, practice, sharing and reflection. Write alongside them. Get to know and value the different voices. Celebrate diversity and withhold judgement. Be prepared for the membership to change over time, but keep the invitations personal and positive, and keep repeating them. Strengthen your group by sharing classroom applications and responses in between your writing meetings. When they are ready, let them begin to choose/suggest activities. Let them shape the meetings.
- **Build up a resource bank.** You might start yourself, by gathering some of the following:

  Small boxes and envelopes, plain and coloured paper, card
  A range of writing implements
  Stapler, scissors, glue, tape
  Collections of postcards, pictures, quotations
  A book box with novels, picture books and poetry
  Magazines and newspapers that can be cut up

CD/DVDs: music, short films or clips

Ephemeral texts – newsletters, tickets, brochures, catalogues and packaging

A props box, hats and scarves, glasses, glove puppets

A collection of objects – buttons, fir cones, jewellery, toys, bric-a-brac, shells, stones

Once the group is established, it's good to ask children to bring and add ideas, texts, objects, pictures, DVDs of their own.

- **Fix a time.** You'll probably need between thirty minutes and three hours, depending on the age and experience of your group. The place needs to suit writing. Groups have preferred plenty of stimulation, refreshments, quiet corners in which to write and a reasonably secluded place in which writing can be read aloud. Some groups use classrooms or libraries.
- **Plan some quick writing exercises** – something to break the ice and 'loosen up the writing muscles'.

If it's a lunchtime club you have to have an activity . . . that they can do while they eat their sandwiches, because otherwise you're running into the difficulty of them trying to write something longhand with one hand and eating their sandwiches with the other, so you need short warm-up activities . . .

(Buckinghamshire group leader)

Suggested activities

- titles, newspaper headlines, opening lines . . . closing lines
- dilemmas
- lists of words, word tiles to arrange
- a simple stem-structure such as 'I like . . .', 'I hate . . .'
- a 'scavenger hunt' of the place you are in –
- freewriting for five minutes without stopping

It is worth agreeing beforehand whether this 'quick writing exercise' will be shared or not – and who, other than you, will lead it. It is often good to have a shared AND a private piece. In that way children can get into the habit of trusting themselves to have a go, and of letting other, more considered, writing 'brew' inside them for a while.

Sometimes it is good to share a few words, but let people keep their more immediate extended thoughts private – at least until you have learnt to trust each other and agreed how people will respond to each other. The duration of these quick writing exercises varies. Timing will depend on the age and appetite of the children. Make sure to allow time for sharing afterwards.

- **Decide the main writing activity.** After a while this is best left to individuals to decide. However, at first, some writers may appreciate some guidance such as:
  - Extend your writing from one of the first exercises – take a word, idea or phrase as a starting point.

- Write in voices or from a particular perspective – *what the woman in the picture was really thinking; how the artefact came to be here; what the tree remembers.*
- Use snatches of overheard conversations or 'found' phrases to launch you into your own writing.
- Find an object/picture/view that interests you and write about it twice, moving your writing position/perspective to do so – once from one point of view, once from another.

- **Agree how you will regather to share.** You will need to establish ground rules; for example, listening to each other attentively and not being afraid just to say thank you. It may be useful to model how to respond to the writing process, rather than the product.

  - Where did you get your ideas from?
  - Which words/parts came easily and where did you struggle?
  - What would you like to do next with your writing?

It can be good to 'silence the critic in your head' and just write quickly without stopping or adjusting or editing too much. Of course, it's valuable to revise and reorder, to pick your words carefully, to expand on certain moments and delete others; even to reorder whole passages for greater clarity and 'patterning'. But there will time for those things later. Trust that the act of writing – 'playing' with writing, if you like – will supply children with answers to those problems which may, to start with, seem uncertain. It's important to explore the medium and trust the process. There will be surprises.

How you share will emerge from individuals' wishes. However, most groups have found it useful, at first, to share thoughts about the process:

1. how easy it was to decide on direction – where the ideas came from
2. what emerged unexpectedly
3. were there places where the writing was hard, or places where the writing flowed more readily – (there may be phrases or ideas that people are ready to share, even if they are not yet ready to read the whole piece)
4. what would the writer like to do next with their writing – with whom they would like to share it, if at all.

When children are ready to share, model attentive listening to tone and content (it helps to hear the writing before you see it). There is more on responding in Chapter 8.

This process may be better in pairs at first, but where it is possible it can be fascinating to read around the group and hear what different writing has emerged during the session from similar stimuli.

Groups of older children have also used these sessions to share writing which has been written outside the group meetings. This may well require much longer discussion and may be more easily managed through individually agreed writing partnerships. Members of the group may agree to take turns to 'present' their writing, or provide copies for others to discuss. Online sharing can help this process happen over time. In such discussion, some groups practise referring to 'the writer' in the third person, while the writer herself/himself listens without commenting. This means that observations can be received less personally. Discussions provide feedback to the writer about how voice, values and effects emerge from choices about structures, patterns, register and vocabulary, and from resonances with other texts.

- **You might like to enhance your group by writing together online.** Most schools have a VLE with separate forums which can be closed except to those who are password approved. This enables all children to see each others' writing and give feedback. This will need to be moderated. A teacher of one Year 6 class said that the biggest boost to children's writing confidence came from appreciation and suggestions from their peer group.
- **When you've met for a while,** ask children what they think the implications are for what they might do in the classroom. Which ideas could be adapted? How do these approaches help with aspects of writing you need to develop, or with writing skills and styles you are encountering in lessons? **It is good to plan a display or an event** – possibly only for the group members and invited friends and family. This may lead you to consider evaluating the effect of the group. It's certainly worth using prompt sheets to collect oral – if not written – evidence of children's experiences and thoughts. It may be that children write better with these approaches than they do in more formal settings. In which case, your evidence will be worth sharing with senior leaders and activities might be extended to more pupils and classes.

Chapter 15

Observations and encounters with children writing

> [W]hat is important is that children in school should write about what matters to them and to someone who matters to them.
>
> (Britton, in Pradl 1982)

When children come to school they bring with them various understandings and misunderstandings of what other people do with writing – in signs, news and entertainment, and in getting by from day to day. Children want to be part of that. They want to find out what writing might do for them – and what they might be able to do with it. They have their own stories too, possibly yet unpacked and still to be assembled. Young children may not be able to articulate this, but they reveal much of it in their behaviour. Of course teachers have responsibility to teach language structures and conventions and provide purposeful contexts for these. But it is by watching and listening that teachers can refine the learning environment, making it as engaging and inclusive as possible, so that all children can become writers.

Teachers in writing groups are looking at how children approach writing, the materials they choose, what they do when they write – and the feedback which they find most helpful. Teachers have used journals to note what happens in classrooms, they have interviewed children and have taken time to observe them when writing. In Chapter 16 we describe ways of thinking about children's writing. In the first Buckinghamshire meeting an extended observation of the teachers as they wrote prompted them to make similar observations in their own classrooms.

This chapter provides glimpses into what has been learnt from the project work which Simon has undertaken with children and their teachers in primary schools, and with students and their teachers in secondary schools and colleges. Please note that all names have been changed in this chapter.

One infant school wants to learn more about how best to nurture children's creative potential. Children arrive in reception class with very different language backgrounds and different degrees of confidence. The school identified seven different children whose 'writing journeys' are being followed over three years. A box of toys and books has been assembled which reflects the topics which the children have already encountered. To this, photographs, recordings, objects and books of the children's own making have been added over time. Having built relationships with the children through monthly visits, the box enabled an adult to play, talk and write alongside the children. By doing so, the children revisited their learning and children from different backgrounds were observed initiating play and responding to prompts. The school wanted to discover what guided children's composition, and what informed their sense of story.

Even before children can transcribe stories of their own, the nature of their play and oral storytelling is full of narrative elements. They:

- repeat actions and sequences which give pleasure
- instinctively overlay actions with sound and song and voice
- draw on events in their lives, and on rhymes and stories that they know
- create characters from objects, toys and puppets
- return to favourite objects, movements and places
- seek to apply logic, cause and consequence
- relate to others through the pleasures of these negotiations.

These can all be strengthened by instruction, by collaborative practice and by cultivating a responsive audience. As children inhabit these worlds in their play, so the language and attitudes of these encounters begin to shape the children from the inside out, reappearing in conversations and stories. Amadeo made up a story using a clockwork chicken, a seed box, some plastic mini-beasts and two glove puppets, a spider and a lamb. He used a mixture of speech and puppetry to tell his story and rang a bell to signal different actions and parts of the story. Amadeo wrote down no words but clearly he can:

- import and connect elements of his own life and understanding into a new story (his own understanding of animals and relationships)
- move in and out of role (swift changes of voice to match character and mood)
- direct, explain and interpret action (explaining the chicken's actions, using the bell for different purposes)
- wrestle with and resolve problems and inconsistencies of narrative (deciding when to continue or when to restart story).

One powerful thing we have learnt about the encouragement of early writers is that we need to listen and to notice without judging. There will, of course be other times when we need to give advice and make judgments. The teacher's skill lies in knowing which to do when.

In another primary school, teachers wanted to learn how writing notebooks, used regularly alongside their play and work, might give children the chance to practise self-expression and to write alongside their teachers. Through play, talk, drawing and mark making, children from all backgrounds enjoyed safe, independent spaces and books.

Zoe (Year 1) loves fairy stories and regularly dresses up as a princess. It is January and she is eagerly retelling the story of *Hansel and Gretel* by writing in a small book. She is sitting at a table next to her friends. She grips her pencil between the third and fourth fingers of her hand, and steadies her book with her left hand. Occasionally she looks up to watch her teacher's interactions with the other children, or to ask about a new word. She crouches back over her writing and twines her pigtail with her left hand. Then she checks off letters on the table word map, changing her initial choice of the word 'house' to the word 'home'.

In another book (her writing notebook), Zoe is free to write what she wishes. She chooses to intersperse repeated retellings of favourite stories (*Rapunzel, Snow White* and *Cinderella*) with lists of her friends – not only who is 'in' or 'out' this week – but who might be having a school lunch. Each retelling shows her becoming more confident with story patterns and returning again and again to wrestle with the injustices in Cinderella's life. The lists are in imitation of her teacher, who modelled for Zoe that writing was an important daily business. Zoe says that her teacher and her father have helped her most with her writing. One of the school's findings was that the writing notebooks encouraged previously reluctant writers, made children more relaxed about sharing their writing with each other, and made them orally more confident.

In a third primary school, to develop children's voice and independence, the headteacher wanted all children to keep writing journals and for the teachers to write too. There was a monthly parents' writing group. Simon supported the school and worked closely with identified Year 3 children.

At home James liked to read football facts and *Doctor Who*. He would make up funny stories about monsters, and wrote in his bedroom, sharing his writing with his friends and his older brother. However, conscious of many misspellings in his writing, James wrote very little at school. He seldom elaborated his thoughts in writing beyond a single sentence: *'Ones I fell of my biek.'*

In January James' teacher introduced writing journals, giving more freedom of choice to her class and, in her feedback, focusing on ideas before technical accuracy. James responded positively: *'I really like writing in my journal, because you can write about anything you want . . . I enjoy it when we're allowed to let our imaginations run wild. Good ideas come to me about the future.'* By June, James had developed confidence to write at greater length and in a distinctive voice. Because of the encouragement he was receiving, he became more determined to check technical features and to self-correct.

> *When Tom went to bed he had a frightfull dream. It was that he was going to be eaten by a wet and slimey crock. He thort it was really scary . . . The next day Tom toled his friend's about his dream but thea just larfed like a bunch of crasy babon's. Tom stormed of. This was sirose.*
>
> (James)

In one comprehensive school, a Year 9 class is taught by an NWP group leader who writes herself. The project is trying to discover what difference this makes. Five Year 9 students have volunteered to review their writing journeys each term with Simon. Each student is interviewed for 20 minutes. In the first term they reflect on their writing habits. In the second term they describe the different demands they face and the support they receive for writing across the curriculum. In the third term they choose a piece of their own writing to read aloud, and then reflect on the process of composition before evaluating their writing and their progress. Then they receive feedback.

In the summer term of 2015, their teacher introduced various dystopian novels to her Year 9 group: *The Hunger Games, Brave New World, The Handmaid's Tale, 1984* and *Clockwork Orange*. These chimed with many of their reading and viewing interests. Many of them are already fans of *Game of Thrones*. The students were given two weeks to plan, discuss and write a 500-word episode from their own imagined dystopia.

One Year 9 student, Jasmine, told how she was influenced by reading (in history) about how soldiers returning from the second world war sometimes received little psychological support in readjusting to civilian life. Jasmine explained that she created a knife-wielding narrator-murderer – not dissimilar to Alex in *Clockwork Orange* – who is in denial about his responsibility for his actions. She says that she wanted to let the reader hear this through the repeated patterns of the narrator's voice: 'pretend . . . pretend . . . I turn almost robotically . . . this was a duty, not a hobby . . . I'm no psychopath . . . (the knife) as if it were mine . . . '

Another Year 9 student, Beth, said that she enjoys anime (*Tokyo Ghoul*) and is increasingly interested in politics. She explained that she had been reading about genetic engineering and the secrecy surrounding mutations. She wants her story to capture what it might be like to grow up knowing that you are 'not normal'. How would such a character tell their story?

Beth reads Simon her writing which has more than a few echoes of Atwood and Orwell – some conscious, some not. In this dystopia, the controlling humans give a number to every mutant, 'as if they were things'. Beth deliberately begins the episode with a disembodied human voice repeating a message over the tannoy. But the mutant-narrator despises her masters. She sneers at their values: 'humans don't kill other humans – unless they fail.' When she arrives at 'the pain room', the mutant-narrator decides to resist the humans, even though she knows, 'If I was caught, I would be immediately put down.' At the critical moment, the narrative slows: 'There was metal. A gun. And a command to shoot . . . '

In discussing her story, Beth explained that the planning she did before writing made it easier for her to 'show not tell'. She wanted the reader to follow the mutant's process of deducing how this dystopia worked: 'I didn't want to add too much information. She's a Voler – from the word "volatile" – but she's not aware that her species has a name. . . . I took that from racism – one race thinks they're superior to another.' Beth shows impressive maturity in the way she conceives of her story and controls the narrative.

These Year 9 students are at ease with metaphor and grammar. They are not patching these things in place in order to 'up-level'. They are not forcing writing into a straitjacket of 'objectives'. They have been given time and responsibility to make their own writing choices. Their writing teacher has established a safe environment for pupils, which is rooted in mutual respect: from her own teachers' writing group, their teacher knows the importance of this. The students have their own writing notebooks; they write together regularly; they discuss the writing process. Their teacher has built on pupils' capabilities and helped them reflect on their progress. Her students have received regular feedback – from each other as well as from her. As a result, they are engaged and motivated and growing in confidence. They are using their writing to explore ideas, connect their reading and shape their values and attitudes – and their progress is immeasurable.

For far too long, from ages 16–18, there was no accredited curriculum course to prepare the 7,000+ students who chose to follow some of the current 450+ undergraduate courses which teach Creative Writing. However, this changed in 2013 with the approval of AQA's Creative Writing qualification. In 2014 there were 2,100 candidates for the AS level.

Most students who choose Creative Writing A level, do so because of long-standing enjoyment in writing from observation and imagination. Often they have been encouraged by previous success in exams and prizes or by their English teachers. Some are attracted by the breadth of reading involved or an interest in honing their skills, some with an eye to a future career in journalism. During interviews with Simon, students reflected that the A level course freedoms are in stark contrast to the prescribed writing at GCSE. They relish the opportunities to read with an author's eyes, to explore their own ideas in writing, to take shared responsibility for the writing of others. They come to respect the character-building disciplines of regular journaling and experimentation, and of submitting their own writing to peer and teacher scrutiny. The following comments are typical:

> I think that personally I've grown as a person because you are very vulnerable and you have to be open to criticism and make sure you don't take it the wrong way. So, for example, when workshopping my pieces people have always given me useful, constructive feedback/criticism.

> I never used to share my work except with my parents, but creative writing gave me such confidence.
>
> (Year 12 creative writing students)

To observe these students sharing and critiquing each other's work is to witness an attentiveness to the tone and movement of language, and a respect for each other and each other's story which is humbling. And all those personal and linguistic skills can be developed across the key stages.

Children and students aged 5–18 have shown us what has helped their writing. Alongside lessons which instruct them in conventions and structures, they attribute their progress in writing to the following factors:

- learning with a teacher who writes, shares and is willing to write alongside them;
- instruction in conventions, structures and disciplines of talk, reading and writing;
- the stimulation derived from reading and studying other practised writers;
- having a writing notebook in which to experiment, regular time to do so and an opportunity to revisit this with their teacher;

- writing outside the classroom with others;
- reading aloud their own writing to their peers, teachers and chosen family members, and learning how to be good response partners themselves;
- receiving sympathetic, non-judgmental responses from their teachers about the content of their writing, and hearing what images and emotions it has provoked.

Reference

Pradl, G.M. (ed.) (1982) *Prospect and Retrospect: Selected Essays of James Britton*. Montclair, NJ: Boynton/Cook.

Chapter 16

Making assessments of writing

> Certainly the point that has come through most clearly to me from other people's comments is the power, the relief and the freedom that children get when their writing is their own, when they have control over the subject matter and know it is not going to be marked. Food for thought I think.
>
> (Primary teacher)

Assessment is about knowing and respecting each child as a writer. It is likely to take into account their roles as speaker, listener and reader in the context of becoming a writer. It is about knowing them precisely in ways that will help us, and them, to know what next steps to take. In this chapter we will place our emphasis on formative assessment in ways that reflect back to Chapter 8 where we considered how response lies at the heart of teaching writing. We think about it both as part of the planning cycle and as an ongoing and explicit dialogue with each writer. We conceive of assessment as something done in partnership with children and with other significant adults. Consequently it is important to think about how the writer's learning is made visible to all interested parties. What evidence might a writer and his teacher collect and what sense might they make of it? We propose that the more frequently a young writer writes for himself, and at the very least with a significant element of choice, the more pertinent the feedback is likely to be. Furthermore, when the writer has control of the writing, they also know, and are in a position to learn, about their process.

> It's difficult to quantify the impact that the creative writing sessions have on students' overall progress. My gut feeling is that, once students feel that they have an investment in their English lessons, through creative writing, they make faster progress. The development of engagement and confidence is obvious in the sessions and students of all abilities are making progress because they have invested more in their learning. Student data tracking this year supports this, and the majority of students who have engaged in creative writing groups are meeting or exceeding their upper quartile targets. My department teaches in mixed ability groups and in last year's GCSE results, the classes that made most progress were those who had participated in creative writing sessions.
>
> (Secondary teacher)

We cannot avoid testing and assessment. What, in the first instance we can avoid, and this is the value of a teachers' writing group, is teaching that is driven entirely by summative assessment. Many children are so hemmed in by instruction that it is well-nigh impossible to make realistic assessments of their writing. Many 'high level' writers, especially in Year 6, have learned to write according to formulae which enable them to meet criteria for a particular level, but not necessarily to write good prose. When writing is judged by the kind of criteria listed in Assessing Pupils' Progress (APP) grids, or by level descriptors, it becomes easy to avoid engaging with the text, with what has actually been written. It is easier still to sideline the writer and so to forget the most important person in the process. If we talk only about the strengths and weaknesses of a text and emphasise suggestions for improvement, we miss opportunities for the kind of development which we discussed in Chapter 8.

We propose:

1. that teachers re-evaluate the use of the portfolio, considering what it might include and how it could be used; and
2. that sharing of and responding to writing and the events that surround writing should be a significant element of the writing curriculum.

The CLPE's Primary Language Record is a good starting point for thinking about how you might structure a portfolio or similar testimony of progress. The Language Record was developed in the 1980s and the CLPE is revisiting it in the light of the most recent National Curriculum for English. Although it began in primary education, it has been developed in North America to embrace secondary years, notably at the University of Austen, Texas, where it is called the Learning Record (http://www.learningrecord. org/). The Language Record is well-embedded in research and embraces the diversity of language and of language learners. It can provide a very firm foundation for principled and thorough record keeping and assessment which will begin to engage with the complexity of the developing writer.

The Language Record has its own clear structure and encompasses all language modes. If you wanted to create a framework to suit your circumstances you could consider including any of the following:

- contributions made by child; parent; teacher; TAs; other involved adults;
- different kinds of writing according to curriculum requirements and decisions made by teacher and writer;
- samples of writing at different stages: e.g. of planning; revising; playfulness; these should be accompanied by notes on the context – how and why the text was written, where, with whom;
- revised writing/writing in class/timed conditions;
- process writing: reflection on different aspects of the writing process;
- writing conferences; sharing writing; peer conferences (Chapter 8);
- notes and reflections on oral feedback;

- written feedback;
- writing interviews – held at regular intervals, perhaps based on the portfolio;
- observations of writers;
- photographs, scans and copies of writing/drawing/small world play/collaborative talk and story-making/notes made as child is drawing/writing;
- audio files of writers reflecting on writing, talking in preparation, articulating process.

The portfolio allows us to make learning visible for the writer and for all those involved in promoting their development. It can capture the subtleties and complexity of becoming a writer and provides the basis for decisions about what to do next.

Documentation comes first. It is through the gathering of evidence through a variety of media (e.g. written and drawn notes, photographs, audio, video, original texts at different stages of composition) that teachers and students can construct an idea of the learning that takes place. In the construction of traces, learning is made visible to teachers and children and becomes the focus for conversation. It 'anchors the social process of learning and invites multiple perspectives, interpretation, and theory building' (Krechevsky *et al.* 2013). Rather than relying on intuitive and possibly biased interpretations, the gathering of evidence and the sharing of it with others, helps us to gain a better understanding of individual writers and of writing as a whole (Barrs & Johnson 1993). It makes possible reciprocal conversations between teachers and learners.

It is important to remember the power of the child's self-chosen writing as the basis for formative assessment and to rethink the different roles and circumstances we can create for formative assessment. Elbow (2000) suggests that we should find ways to 'step out of grading', step 'outside the mentality of judgement'. Having discovered what this means for their own writing, many teachers reserve at least one space in their busy timetables for what they often call 'creative writing' where they are likely to use journals and freewriting, to give children the most choice, and to emphasise sharing and feedback, rather than marking against given criteria.

> After a term of the creative writing sessions, I asked my Year 7 students to write on Post-it notes something that they found difficult or didn't like about writing, and something that they liked about writing, or a reason why they wrote. Almost without exception, the negatives that were identified related to transactional and technical aspects of writing – particular spelling patterns or punctuation that they found difficult. The positive aspects that they identified were all linked to inventing characters and plots, and creativity. When I asked them to make a whole class list of reasons why they write and who they write for, they came up with the following:
>
> Because I have to (not because she was made to, but that she couldn't imagine not writing)
> For myself
> For my friends and family

So that I can invent my own world
To use my imagination
Because I enjoy it

No-one added 'So that I can improve my grade' and 'Because I have to at school', until I raised these ideas. They were then added to the list, but as an obvious afterthought.

(Secondary teacher)

There is no denying the fact that it is not always easy to work in this way, given the current pressures on schools and the characterisation of progress that is in vogue.

Elbow (2000) recognises the value of a whole range of responses and focus for assessment. His 'map of writing', which is a way of considering these, is a four by three grid where there are four kinds of audience on the vertical axis:

1. with authority over the writer
2. peers
3. audience of allies/readers who particularly care for the writer
4. the self alone – private writing

and three kinds of response on the horizontal axis:

1. sharing but no response
2. response but no criticism or evaluation
3. criticism or evaluation

(Elbow 2000: 29)

The map embodies the safety towards risk, easier to harder spectrum, and may lead you to believe, 'elementary to advanced' which is not the case. Draw out the grid for yourself and think about the different conjunctions of audience and kind of response. Writers value and benefit from *all* combinations and will need them at different times. The pity is that most school pupils rarely experience anything other than the audience who has authority and makes an evaluative or critical response. Teachers often do not allow themselves the opportunity to see what a student can do when given freer rein.

In a community of writers, we develop together our understandings of writing and of how individual writers can develop. In the community of the classroom, Michael Armstrong (2006) proposes, young writers should expect to find an audience amongst their peers and their teachers. Part of their growth as writers becomes dependent on the ways they learn to listen and respond to the writing of others. The job of the teacher is to set the conditions and find the possibilities which allow young writers to develop. In order to do so, the teacher must learn to listen and to observe in ways that will inform her actions. Armstrong conceives of the act of reading as an interpretative art. In engaging with what is written and how it emerged, the teacher ascertains what has been achieved and seeks the next steps for the writer.

In classrooms devoted to works and the making of works, interpretation becomes synonymous with assessment and evaluation. To identify with the work, draw out its intention, meditate on its significant form and anticipate the direction of future work is to render the work its due value, whether within the process of learning or as learning's product.

(Armstrong 2006: 180)

Armstrong (2006) defines 'four moments of interpretation' when engaging with children's narratives:

1. Inhabit the work; acknowledge its authority. Believe what is written and work with what the writer is offering.
2. Step back a little from the text. Draw out the work's narrative intention both as the author has consciously recognised it and implicit within the text. Explore the language; the interplay of form and content; consider the text's underlying significance, the light it sheds on life, including the author's own sense of life.
3. Independently, or with fellow readers and writers, re-describe, represent your understanding of the work. Share perceptions; speculate; ask questions.
4. Look to the future that is implicit in the work of the present both of the individual and the collective. The teacher must consider what might be the next step. What has she learned from her reading of the text that indicates what might best help the writer? Next steps may be decided in response to one child's writing. However, often there is a pattern in the work of the group which will prompt the teacher to think about what to do next. As they become used to this way of working with writing, the class, also, will think about next steps – and increasingly the class will contribute to the development of writing.

Focus of attention may be:

- development of verbal or grammatical skills in the light of the existing equilibrium of skill and purpose;
- introduction of new genres or techniques – perhaps implicit in the works children have made;
- literature which responds to the work: novels, poetry, folk tales, picture books, literary non-fiction;
- further exploration of the subject matter, the human predicaments confronted in narrative form;
- the extension of the work through other art forms – drama, dance, music, art, history.

In looking forward, the distinctive role of teachers is to bring all their accumulated knowledge to bear on the task of helping the class to move ahead. Teachers are both representatives and critics of the wider culture. Such an approach recognises the importance of the collective influence of the classroom. Young writers and readers learn from each other and create a culture of reading and writing.

Such close reading and the skill of deciding how best to help writers grow develops with careful thought in the company of others. The teachers' writing group provides the locus for teachers to develop their skills of listening, reading, interpreting and responding; the opportunity to make close readings of children's texts within that community of learners. Cross-phase groups have the opportunity to look closely at children's writing across the age range (from 4–18 in some cases). Teachers bring in examples of children's writing and present them for consideration. Sometimes we look at the patterns and surprises we notice across a range of ages. Sometimes one piece of writing will take up all the time we have. In reading closely, in listening with attention, we get to the heart of teaching writing. In order to do this job well, we value the experience of writing and reflecting with others.

> I've always enjoyed children's writing but sometimes you just get used to it, seeing it every day. I love how writing teachers reminds me how amazing the things my pupils do every day are. I'll bring something in I think is kind of cool and everyone will be amazed and it will make me feel like I'm doing a decent job! Or I'll take a learning moment, the kind I witness many times daily, but then analyse it for writing teachers and realise just how deep and complex the learning is.
>
> (Early Years teacher)

This approach to children's writing owes much to the work of Armstrong (2006), D'Arcy (1999/2000?), Harvard's Project Zero (Krechevsky *et al.* 2013) and the work of Prospect School (Carini 2001; Himley 2000). The descriptive review of the child provides us with an attitude of mind that is open and inquiring in terms of what young writers reveal. The emphasis on children's works as acts of making meaning and discovery does stand in contrast to assessment which takes a narrow view of the written product. An emphasis on grammatical constructions and strict notions of form gives rise to forms of assessment which focus solely on surface features and overlook meaning. Assessment of writing that has been set within strict boundaries and produced within a system will be of how well the writer has performed in that system, not necessarily how well they write. Close consideration of students' own texts and acts of writing provide us with a richer, more pertinent understanding of progress and achievement.

> What strikes me most in our current cultural moment is how preoccupied people are with institutional evaluation, assessment, and testing of all sorts, and how much one-dimensional scores and grades are a tail that wags teaching and learning.
>
> (Elbow 2000)

Fifteen years on and the tail is still vigorously wagging the dog. Certainly in English schools, the measure of writing depends to such an extent on the inclusion of quantifiable grammatical features that teachers, and therefore children, are so disconnected from the act of writing itself that the chance to learn its pleasures and affordances is often completely missed. Teachers' writing groups create the possibility of re-articulating what development as a writer might look like. The issue of assessment, both summative and formative, is one that teachers of writing need to address as a matter of urgency. We wish to continue to develop understanding of the kinds of assessment that are fair and constructive, and which properly reflect a child's skills and understanding as a writer.

References

Armstrong, M. (2006) *Children Writing Stories*. Maidenhead: Open University Press.

Barrs, M. & Johnson, G. (1993) *Record-keeping in the Primary School*. London: Hodder & Stoughton.

Carini, P. F. (2001) *Starting Strong: A Different Look at Children, Schools, and Standards*. New York & London: Teachers College Press.

D'Arcy, P. (1999/2000) *Two Contrasting Paradigms for the Teaching and Assessment of Writing: A Critique of Current Approaches to the National Curriculum*. Sheffield: NATE.

Elbow, P. (2000) *Everyone Can Write: Essays Toward a Hopeful Theory of Writing and Teaching Writing*. New York & Oxford: Oxford University Press.

Himley, M, with Carini, P. F. (eds.) (2000) *From Another Angle: Children's Strengths and School Standards: The Prospect Center's Descriptive Review of the Child*. New York & London: Teachers College Press.

Krechevsky, M., Mardell, B., Rivard, M. & Wilson, D. (2013) *Visible Learners: Promoting Reggio-inspired Approaches in All Schools*. San Fransico, CA: Jossey-Bass.

Chapter 17

Writing groups – from community to classroom and from classroom to community

We have found that teachers' writing groups can help to restore agency and authority to writing teachers. What teachers learn in the groups informs how they go on to teach in their classrooms. They return to their schools inwardly restored and empowered. With their professional authority 'rebooted', they can start to cultivate a wider writing community in and around their classrooms. Many teachers have run workshops to share their understandings with colleagues. On a school training day, an NWP group leader, and secondary head of English, offered her colleagues a writing workshop. She was delighted to find that colleagues came willingly from across the curriculum; private writers 'came out'. Similarly, another NWP teacher in an Ilford school has started a weekly after-school writing group which is attended by a range of professionals from across the curriculum: teaching assistants, support staff, librarians, and teachers from technology, Modern Foreign Languages (MFL) and English.

Such cross-curricular engagement is encouraging. The NWP (USA) is a cross-curricular writing project and rightly so. *Thinking Writing* at Queen Mary University of London champions writing as a fundamental learning process and is interdisciplinary in conception (Mitchell 2010). An interdisciplinary project at Coventry University explored the cross-curricular benefits of storytelling. Undergraduates in law, social sciences and medical studies were asked to compose stories to illustrate their understandings of concepts. Students became more fully engaged, deepened their learning through the application of their imaginations, and thereby gained a more secure grasp of complex issues (Morris & Kelly 2015).

Teachers have also run practical writing sessions for parents. To illustrate the fuller affordances of writing, one primary school advertised a *Writing Breakfast*. Counter to the school's expectations, attendance exceeded the previous *Reading Breakfast*. The session invited parents to write alongside their children and understand better that only some of the writing challenge was technical. For half an hour before school, over coffee and croissants, parents stayed to experience a writing workshop. In both starting and sharing writing, most parents found their children less inhibited than they were. Parents quickly understood the riskiness of the writing enterprise, the importance of trust and encouragement, and were grateful to their children for the opportunity to collaborate. For one single mother of two, this was a rare chance to attend fully to her son's developing ideas while the teacher, quite literally, held the baby. Parents commented how rare, and pleasurable, it had been to 'be creative' alongside their own children.

In November 2010, as part of his work as a local authority advisor, Simon decided to explore whether children, teachers and other writers in the Princes Risborough community, might benefit from working alongside each other on a community writing project in Buckinghamshire. He invited the well-known author, Kevin Crossley-Holland, to be the figurehead of this project. Kevin had just published *The Hidden Roads*, a memoir of his own writing 'journey' which began on the outskirts of Princes Risborough, at the foot of Whiteleaf Hill. This crossing place of various Neolithic pathways and Roman roads, had retained a significance for him, reflected in his choice of *At the Crossing Places* as the title for one of his books in the 'Arthur' trilogy. His childhood apprehension of the great beech trees on the hilltop became, in his fiction, presences speaking of earlier times.

Over the weeks that followed the launch of the project in the secondary school, Kevin worked with pupils, teachers and parents in many of the fifteen local primary and secondary schools. Separately and sometimes together, adults and children wrote about those places which were significant to them. Young writers wrote about the hills and hedgerows, cupboards, passageways and stadia, as well as more intimate dens and attics, real and imagined.

> My special place is a tree which has a door. The door is an arch. My tree is called Mr Dar Smith. I can climb it and I can peel the wood.
>
> (Max, Year 2)

> I feel the gentle breeze from the wind hit me softly. When I look at the sunset I get a powerful feeling that I belong right here where I'm standing in the middle of the huge field full with secrets, dreams and hopes . . .
>
> (Holly, Year 6)

Simon worked alongside Kevin in schools. Simon also set up and led a writing group for interested adults in the town library, and worked with the adult facilitators and residents in a local Fremantle home for the elderly. The local authority provided a website on which progress could be recorded and children's and adults' writing could be safely shared. They undertook a mixed age 'writing walk' which finished by writing and sharing in someone's kitchen. In March 2011, an anthology of writing, *Chalk Road*, which celebrated the local population's witness of place, was published. The age range of the writers included was 5–98.

> Yes! Yes! screamed the children, as fears of dangerous predators were instantly cast aside and they sped off the path in search of suitable fallen branches. I stumbled after them as best I could, scrambling over moss-covered, toppled tree trunks and ducking under treacherous low branches which clutched at my clothes and even at my skin . . .
>
> (Bill)

The terracotta tiles judder slightly under the rumble of the doll's pram wheels and the air is sharp with the smell of hot rust from our grandmother's geraniums on their high windowsill.

(Lynda)

(For more detail visit the website: http://j.mp/significantplaces)

In May 2012, as a result of this community writing project, Kevin led another with schools and adults in north Norfolk. This culminated in the publication of a community anthology entitled *Between the Land and the Sea*. Such projects connect communities in a creative endeavour which is about validating their experiences and feelings rather than about proving levels of control of genres and conventions. They draw on the resources of the community, and help pupils see writing as a meaningful pursuit beyond exams and classrooms and commercial application.

In 2014, Simon interviewed five members from different local writing groups in Bedford to find out what schools could learn from them. There is a National Association of Writers' Groups (NAWG). Some adult writing groups are led by a published tutor who aims to help writers get into print and exist to help writers get published. However, many writing groups exist for social purposes, providing a community in which writing can be a valued way of being in the world.

The motivation of their members seemed to share three characteristics:

1. the companionship of a trusted forum where their voices can be heard – by reading their work aloud, they discover how authentically and effectively they have written;
2. a stiffening of resolve to submit to the discipline of shaping experience and ideas in words, through being regularly challenged and encouraged to write and share;
3. a privileged perspective into other writers' insights and voices, and the chance to respond and encourage others.

For many there had been a transforming event around the age of fifteen or sixteen which had turned them on to writing for life. Often it was suddenly recognising their teacher as 'someone who thinks and feels about words the way I do'. Sometimes an inspirational teacher had introduced them to the words of a poet: 'I was bowled away by (hearing Ted Hughes' style) – a means of expression that I would want to use in some way . . . this seemed to be a way I could talk about experience (whereas other poets spoke in distant voices.)' (Interviews with members of five adult writing groups in Bedford, May–June 2014.)

Some mentioned discovering the benefits of solitary journaling as they moved through the crises of a more independent life: '. . . a journal was somewhere I could work important things out, where I could be present and private, reveal myself to myself in a forum in which I dared – holding events which were momentous and distilling understandings that were important. Writing was a way of taking care of that.'

Although the pressures of work and family often reduced the time for writing, many were still grateful for those schoolteachers who had helped them wrestle with writing, and had cultivated in them a habit of 'discovery writing' to which they returned on their own, or with their group, whenever they could:

You can discover who you are through writing.

Faced with a blank piece of paper, everyone is equal – back at square zero.

The more opportunities for creativity, the more people can find themselves.

(Poetry) is good for the soul . . . you become better at understanding the world and yourself.

One of the group organisers, a published poet who has set up regular 'open mic' events, stressed the importance to any writer of hearing how written words sounded aloud. 'Things start to gel when you get a kind of sound in your head and it takes you forward. Sometimes you can't hear yourself; it's a kind of deafness . . . a poem is not finished until you've road-tested it on an audience – can this live for somebody else?' He recommended asking someone else to read your poem aloud as 'a helpful way of reflecting and giving distance'.

Some of these adults' writing groups have 'education officers', and many contain adults who offer their services to schools. Schools should not restrict writing visitors just to those who are published or famous. It is clearer now than ever with the amount of writing which we all do, on or offline, that writing is the habit of the many rather than the preserve of the few. And the reasons for why and how things get published needs to be opened up and not remain a secret garden. For their encouragement and edification, teachers as well as children need to meet other adults within their own community who choose to write and are prepared to share their enthusiasms, their methods and their products.

Visits to school by published authors are hugely valuable and provide great inspiration to young writers. Another adult's perspective, uncircumscribed by tests and 'progress measures', is refreshing. Often, and unsurprisingly, the short duration of a writer's residence means that freedoms are encouraged more than rules, immediacy is prized over long editing, and, since writing is heard more often than seen, the scales tip away from secretarial skills towards fresh expression and insight. Because school assessment and inspection is so heavily reliant on lasting marks made by children and students on paper, writing is more often seen than heard in schools. However, when teachers – and visiting authors – encourage pupils to read their work aloud to each other – and to respond and reflect, their writing improves. In such less inhibiting circumstances, children and student writers are more likely to discover a more personalised 'flow'. Redrafting which might have been tedious and counterproductive before, becomes interactive and informed by the writer's own ears as well as their eyes.

NAWE's 2010 report, *Class Writing*, reported on the 'Writers-in-Schools Ecology'. The report is keen to emphasise that the effect of a writer's residential varies according to the context – what work precedes and follows, as well as how the visit itself is conducted. There needs to be a respectful partnership between the writer and teacher in which each can learn from the other and compromise.

In 2014, when writer and poet, Berlie Doherty visited an NWP school with established writing practices, she was impressed by the readiness to write of both children and adults. As a result the sessions were productive. Teachers and teaching assistants wrote alongside the children, the children kept their own writing notebooks and saw themselves as writers. This was not the first time a published author had visited the school.

Mutual preparation ensures a more lasting legacy and avoids the unquestioning repetition of bad practice. For example, writers Anne Fine and Philip Pullman condemned the entrenched practice of redrafting which had become, in some schools, an automatic and perfunctory activity of 'up-levelling', more likely to put children off writing than improve their 'performance'. Creatively handled, in a context where everyone writes freely and regularly in a writing notebook, and where the 'ownership' of writing processes is more democratic, reflective editing is more likely to succeed. Rather than advocate any scheme or fixed sequence, the report refers to a loose set of activities which could be practised before and after an author visit and which would embed healthier and more inclusive writing approaches: 'Adventuring; Expanding; Editing; Completing . . . It's hard for anyone to understand the purpose of writing or find any joy in it if you don't allow for the full journey' (Owen & Munden 2010).

Sadly and ironically, in the education climate of 2015, the blunter method of 'rigorously' chasing 'performance targets' seems repeatedly to limit the potential of children and cramp the creative style of teachers. What *Class Writing* reported in 2010, is even truer in 2015: teachers perceive a lack of permission for enriching contacts with artists.

The report ends by quoting Andrew Motion's *Guardian* article of 7 October 2003:

> By making writing a central part of their school experience, we offer pupils the chance to make heartening discoveries of themselves, and to deepen and diversify their connection with the world. If they produce important works of art, we shall all be grateful. If they don't, we'll still be grateful. They'll have learned what it is to be educated in the round.

References

Crossley-Holland, K. (2001) *At the Crossing Places.* London: Orion Children's.

Crossley-Holland, K. (2009) *The Hidden Roads: A memoir of childhood.* London: Quercus.

Mitchell, S. (2010) 'Now you don't see it; now you do. Writing made visible in the university.' In *Arts and Humanities in Higher Education*, 9(2), 133–148.

Morris, A. & Kelly, T. (2015) 'Creative Assessment: Writing Stories as Coursework Across the Disciplines.' In *Writing in Education*, Issue Number 65, Spring 2015, 27–32.

Owen, N. & Munden, P. (2010) *Class Writing: A NAWE Research Report into the Writers-in-Schools Ecology.* York: NAWE.

Chapter 18

What's in it for my school?

School leaders in England recognise the importance of pupils' progress in tested writing skills. It is a key Ofsted measure in determining their schools' effectiveness. So teachers have to have high expectations. Leaders also know that a teacher who can engage pupils with creative writing will be contributing to pupils' spiritual development, defined by Ofsted as:

- sense of enjoyment and fascination in learning about themselves, others and the world around them
- use of imagination and creativity in their learning
- willingness to reflect on their experiences.

(Ofsted 2014)

When teachers 'do something creative' – or let pupils take ownership of a purposeful challenge, activity or enquiry – they are often surprised by what the children are capable of. So having genuinely 'high expectations' of pupils involves being open-minded rather than fixated on particular destinations.

An NWP teacher in an infant school recorded changes of attitude and linguistic control that occurred in Year 1 class after she had introduced the regular flexible use of writing journals for 20–40 minutes a week. The children's responses reflect pleasure in freer writing regimes, as well as a growing understanding of how writing can help them:

It doesn't matter if I don't finish it now, I can go back later. I can write what I want.

I like writing all my ideas down. It helps me remember everything.

She had underestimated the children's writing capacity: 'reluctant writers' were not reluctant towards writing, but to compulsion and judgment. Furthermore, she recognised that the benefits of journals extended beyond progress in writing attainment. Levels of anxiety were reduced, risk-taking increased, children spoke more articulately and listened more attentively because they were writing about what mattered to them. With a view of themselves as 'writers' the children developed a new curiosity about how books had been 'written'. And their standards of reading rose.

In 2014–2015, in order to understand how NWP writing teachers were raising standards in more than merely tested skills, Simon interviewed headteachers in both primary and secondary schools. These headteachers wanted to improve the writing environment for young writers, and both were evaluating the effects of employing teachers who wrote themselves.

In a community primary school which Ofsted had judged 'outstanding', the head-teacher introduced a teachers' writing group as part of a way of refreshing learning. This corresponded to the sole recommendation for improvement from the 2014 Ofsted report: 'Further enhance the curriculum so that the pupils gain an even greater passion for learning in and out of school'.

The headteacher had independently observed that teachers as well as pupils relied too heavily on the safety of familiar formulae rather than taking informed risks. Planning needed to be more ambitious – shaped around more open questions and bigger ideas, rather than simply aiming for required targets. Teachers needed to cultivate pupils' ability to learn collaboratively as well independently. Assessment needed to look beyond levels of attainment and recognise pupils' stamina, engagement, resilience, perseverance, confidence, teamwork and independence of thinking.

The teaching of writing had sometimes become preoccupied with secretarial features. Teachers were conscientious and did not want to forfeit hard-won gains by allowing pupils too much freedom to experiment. They felt nervous of not guiding children or holding their hands towards approved destinations. Guided writing could sometimes be over-heavily modelled 'Big Write' sessions and tended to use unnegotiated external stimuli which did not allow pupils to draw freely on their genuine experiences and inner resources. Some teachers were relatively inexperienced in the teaching of creative writing and felt unsure about how to manage freewriting, writing notebooks, writing alongside pupils or developing pupils as response partners in the classroom. So the headteacher decided to engage teachers with an NWP writing workshop.

Afterwards a writing group was set up to support those teachers who wished to explore their own writing and to discuss changes in classroom practice. Ten teachers from Years 1 to 6 trialled approaches with their classes and introduced pupils' writing journals.

> [N]ow I make sure that they see me writing. And it's really helped with the atmosphere . . . and just sharing our thought processes.
>
> (Year 5 teacher)

Knowing more about the writing process has given teachers the confidence to 'allow' and nurture more creative spaces for pupils. They allow pupils more time to practise, experiment and reflect. Teachers now respond more to the content and process of pupils' writing, not just its structures. There is more open discussion in class of the effects.

All teachers report on a significant rise in pupil engagement and that pupils are willingly writing in greater depth and detail. Pupils now see themselves as writers, and are more prepared to work on improving the quality of their writing because they have more ownership and understanding of the methods, contents and quality. They are supported by rules but not bound by them. Their writing demonstrates a new commitment, and, through experimentation, an increased surety of tone and control of form.

The school's main findings:

1. Teachers who write together discover aspects of writing which help them improve their own teaching of writing.
2. By reflecting on differences between a teachers' writing group and their classroom contexts, teachers learn important messages about reader-writer relationships.
3. Less confident pupils grow as writers when their teacher writes alongside them.
4. Pupils, particularly boys, benefit from regular opportunities to write freely (30 minutes a week).

In a city secondary school which was judged by Ofsted to be requiring improvement, the headteacher is committed to employing a teacher who writes. Not only does this give the school the confidence and capacity to offer AQA's Creative Writing AS and A level, but it informs and liberates the writing culture. The NWP teacher has opened up the writing process for students and given them more time, skill and confidence to undertake independent creative writing. This helps to address some of the areas identified as needing improvement in the school's previous Ofsted report:

- Not all teachers have sufficiently high expectations and do not plan lessons which challenge students according to their assessed needs, particularly those that are more able.
- Students are not enabled to understand how to improve their work and take responsibility for improving their progress.
- There are not enough opportunities in lessons for students to talk about their work and to work independently. Teachers do not consistently use questioning to challenge thinking and move learning on.

Over the last few years, the number of students arriving with English as an additional language has risen to 43 per cent of the intake. This recent change reinforces the need for the school to provide stability and enrichment in language provision.

Above all, the headteacher wants writing to be treated as a tool to help students think independently, and to express their own thoughts accurately and fluently. He acknowledges the limitations of 'teaching to the test' which will not necessarily encourage or reward all that different students are capable of. He is, therefore, keen to cultivate teachers who can build students' confidence and delight in writing and reading.

He recognises that examinations now require students to demonstrate their ability to write more considered and lengthy responses. He therefore wants to promote opportunities for dialogue, reflection and personalisation in the learning of writing. He sees these as not only essential for developing secure learning 'connections', but also as skills which underpin coherent and confident speech. He is convinced that by regularly expressing their own thoughts in writing – however tentative and incomplete these may be – students' speech becomes more composed, articulate and confident in conversations, debates and interviews.

This philosophy is informed by his understanding of students' backgrounds and his wish to respond to their needs. Where students are cocooned by technology, over-reliant on visual stimulation, or lack regular dialogue with others, their ability to process understanding or to cultivate expression is restricted. He is convinced that such isolation limits students' vocabulary, ideas, arguments and values.

Recent rises in exam results and student participation give him confidence to think that his policy is working. He is committed to investing in the continuing professional development of writing teachers because of the more inclusive practices they promote, the greater engagement of students and the increased rates of progress.

Our evidence suggests that the teacher who takes time to write and learn alongside her own pupils will make more difference to the quality of learning in a school, and increase pupils' independence and resilience more than if they had single-mindedly been preoccupied with tested skills.

Reference

Ofsted (2014) *Ofsted Inspecting Schools: Handbook for Inspectors.* First published 19 September 2014, updated 19 December 2014. Ofsted. Retrieved from: https://www.gov.uk/government/publications/school-inspection-handbook, accessed July 2015.

Chapter 19

Afterword

Becoming part of the conversation

Writing, despite its seeming permanence on the page, is always provisional. The late Mike Hayhoe, who lectured at UEA, used to relate how, at a reading in King's Lynn, the poet Stephen Spender took out a pencil, mid-poem, and revised a line. Writing requires courage. It is, also, we would argue, hugely satisfying as a tool for thinking, a way of connecting, a source of laughter, a way of making meaning. We should like all teachers of writing to enjoy writing as much as writing teachers do. We should like those they teach to find what it is about writing that works for them.

We have learned in the course of writing this that we are at a point where we as teachers really can take ownership of the teaching of writing.

We have learned that teachers who write have a rich, complex, nuanced understanding of writing and that children who work with them love writing. However, we haven't finished thinking about writing, or been able to properly articulate, in all its fullness, what it is that writing teachers do. This is what gives teachers' writing groups their energy: we want to know more.

There is so much that needs to be researched about writing and about how we teach it. Teachers' writing groups provide a home base for teachers choosing to be inquirers in the classroom. Here questions are asked, evidence sought and theories probed. Often, even before questions are framed, careful observation prompts teachers to re-evaluate, to re-consider. Ann Berthoff (1981) suggests that research means 'looking – and looking again'; we should look again at what is happening in classrooms. In looking again, in reflecting alone and with others, we re-learn. We become more complete teachers. Teachers' writing groups foster authoritative practitioners who are willing to work alongside others to develop practice. They are well-placed to work with universities as partners in research and in teacher education.

Teachers' writing groups are good for individuals and good for an emerging pedagogy of writing. They are good for children. They are strong, mutually supportive and professional communities of practice. Their singular strength comes from writing itself. A teachers' writing group shapes professional identities. Teachers who write for themselves and with others have the capacity to reveal to those they teach what it is to belong to a community of writers.

If learning is a matter of identity, then identity itself is an educational resource. It can be brought to bear through relations of mutuality to address a paradox of learning: if one needs an identity of participation in order to learn, yet needs to learn in order to acquire an identity of participation, then there seems no way to start. Addressing this most fundamental paradox is what, in the last analysis, education is about. In the life-giving power of mutuality lies the miracle of parenthood, the essence of apprenticeship, the secret to the generational encounter, the key to the creation of connections across boundaries of practice: a frail bridge across the abyss, a slight breach on the law, a small gift of undeserved trust – it is almost a theorem of love that we can open our practices and communities to others (newcomers, outsiders), invite them into our own identities of participation, let them be what they are not, and thus start what cannot be started.

(Wenger 1999: 277)

We would like you to find time to write for yourself.

We would like you to join a group with whom to write and share writing.

We would like you to have fun and think hard.

We would like you to record, rethink, articulate what you are learning about how children become writers and your role in that.

We would like you to ask the hard questions and seek some answers in your own teaching and with other writing teachers.

We invite you to join us in setting up groups; researching teaching and learning; challenging the current status quo.

This book is a product of where we are now, but much more importantly looks forward to where teachers' writing groups can take us.

References

Berthoff, A. (1981) *The Making of Meaning: Metaphors, Models and Maxims for Writing Teachers.* Upper Montclair, NJ: Boynton/Cook.

Wenger, E. (1999) *Communities of Practice.* Cambridge: CUP.

Chapter 20

Books and websites

We are often asked for ideas for reading. This list should be a good start for group leaders and the interested writing teacher. For more links and suggestions, look at The National Writing Project (UK) website: www.nwp.org.uk.

Books

Anderson, L. (2006) *Creative Writing: A Workbook with Readings*. London: Routledge. This book covers all genres. Its exercises and discussion points have been popular amongst writing groups.

Andrews, R. & Smith, A. (2011) *Developing Writers: Teaching and Learning in the Digital Age*. Maidenhead: Open University Press. This book is at the cutting edge of thinking about teaching writing. It endorses teachers' writing groups and includes a consideration of multi-modal texts, of the different literacies with which young people engage, especially beyond school, and the notion of writing as design. You may be interested in Richard Andrews' proposal for a National Writing Project: Andrews, R. (2008) *The Case for a National Writing Project for Teachers*. Reading: CfBT Education Trust.

Armistead, C. (2012) 'Introduction.' In *Write*. London: Guardian Books. A collection of advice and maxims by contemporary writers.

Bassot, B. (2013) *The Reflective Journal*. London: Palgrave Macmillan. Many people like using this well-focused book which provides a reassuringly practical introduction to reflective practice. Bassot offers a variety of ways that a practitioner might choose to write reflectively.

Bolton, G. (2014) *Reflective Practice: Writing and Professional Development*. London: Sage. This is an immensely practical and well-researched book grounded in the author's long experience of working on reflective practice with many different practitioners. It includes thought-provoking chapters on why we might write and about different ways of using writing as a tool for thinking. Many ideas to support reflective writing.

Brande, D. (1996) *Becoming A Writer*. Basingstoke: Macmillan. This book, first published in 1932, is something of a classic and is chiefly about ways of getting started and overcoming resistance to writing. It is where the idea of 'morning pages' comes from – that is, writing immediately after one wakes as a routine and then moving on to finding regular times for writing.

Burroway, J., with Stuckey-French. E. (2007) *Writing Fiction: A Guide to Narrative Craft*. New York & London: Pearson Longman. Combines excellent readings with thought-provoking exercises which cover many aspects of narrative fiction.

Carnell, E., MacDonald, J., McCallum, B. & Scott, M. (2008) *Passion and Politics: Academics Reflect on Writing for Publication*. London: Institute of Education, University of London. This brilliant collection of interviews with academic writers is of particular interest to those writing in the university or who want to write about theory and practice. It is a celebration of writing, thinking and learning.

Clark, R. P. (2013) *How to Write Short*. New York, NY: Little, Brown and Company. This book is crammed with humour and good advice about writing short texts. Each, short, chapter contains writing prompts.

Cowan, A. (2011) *The Art of Writing Fiction*. Harlow: Pearson Education. This is a great book. Writing groups enjoy using it. Individual writers have found its very good advice encouraging. It also very clearly acknowledges the part that autobiography plays in the writing of fiction.

Dymoke, S. (2003) *Drafting and Assessing Poetry: A Guide for Teachers*. London: Paul Chapman. This is a comprehensive and well-researched book written by an experienced teacher and poet. It is immensely practical and could form the backbone for any plans to teach poetry, especially if you feel less confident about this than you would like. It includes sections on using poet's drafts, on drafting and redrafting and on response to writing.

Dymoke, S., Barrs, M., Lambirth, A. & Wilson, A. (2014) *Making Poetry Happen: Transforming the Poetry Classroom*. London: Bloomsbury Academic. Essential reading. It is the most up-to-date and vibrant book about teaching poetry we know. It is practical and principled. The thinking here chimes easily with the work of teachers' writing groups and will provide nourishment and inspiration.

Elbow, P. (1973) *Writing Without Teachers*. London & New York: Oxford University Press. This is a useful book for those starting a group. Exactly as the title suggests, it is written for people who wish to write together and includes chapters on freewriting, writing process and responding, and ideas for writing.

Foden, G. (ed.) (2011) *Body of Work: 40 Years of Creative Writing at UEA*. Woodbridge, Suffolk: Full Circle Editions. This is an absorbing collection of pieces by writers connected with the creative writing course at UEA. More than anything, reading any one of these pieces requires the teacher of writing to think differently about writing and to feel comfortable with the unexpected.

Geraghty, M. (2009) *The Five-minute Writer: Exercise and Inspiration in Creative Writing in Five Minutes a Day*. Oxford: How To Books. Does what it says on the tin. So useful when you are short of either.

Goldberg, N. (1986) *Writing Down the Bones: Freeing the Writer Within*. Boston & London: Shambhala. Goldberg, N (1991) *Wild Mind: Living the Writer's Life*. London: Rider. These two are classics, particularly *Writing Down the Bones*. They appear on many reading lists and provide a combination of reflection, writing life advice and ideas for writing. Dip in and out of them.

Goldberg, N. (2007) *Old Friend from Far Away. The Practice of Writing Memoir.* New York & London: Free Press. Natalie Goldberg writes with great warmth and encouragement. It is possible to take ideas from anywhere in the book or to use it as the basis for quite an intense approach to writing memoir. One of the things Goldberg does well is to suggest ideas from an unusual angle so that one doesn't think about one's long, dull life and go into a quick decline. Her approach to writing memoir provides prompts for the individual and for the workshop leader that are both reassuring and surprising.

Harwayne, S. (2001) *Writing Through Childhood: Rethinking Process and Product.* Portsmouth, NH: Heinemann. Shelley Harwayne is the headteacher of an elementary school in New York where children and teachers are writers from the youngest to the oldest. The book benefits from Harwayne's enthusiasm and commitment and the fact that the examples of children's writing come from every age and from children over time, from kindergarten to sixth grade. This is an immensely practical book, offering specific ideas and well understood principles for teaching writing.

Heard, G. (1989) *For the Good of the Earth and the Sun: Teaching Poetry.* Portsmouth, NH: Heinemann. Although this has a focus on poetry its advice is relevant to most writing groups. It is based on the writer's experience as a writer in schools in New York. The chapters on revising and conferencing are particularly recommended.

King, S. (2000) *On Writing: A Memoir of the Craft.* London: Hodder & Stoughton. This is a page-turner. Stephen King writes about his life as a writer and his emphasis is on the craft. The book is filled with stories and with good advice and observations about writing.

Koch, K. (1970) *Wishes, Lies, and Dreams: Teaching Children to Write Poetry.* New York: Harper & Row. Another classic title, alongside Koch's *Rose, Where Did You Get That Red?* (1990) London: Vintage. These ideas come from Koch's work in New York schools and are based on simple prompts for writing that can work well both as part of collaborative and individual writing. Adults and children find the ideas liberating. They certainly offer the potential for a different way of thinking.

Krementz, J. (1996) *The Writer's Desk.* New York: Random House. A collection of photographs of writers at their desks – or wherever they usually write. Each photograph is accompanied by reflections on writing by the author pictured. We mention using this book in Chapter 11.

Lamott, A. (1995) *Bird by Bird: Some Instructions on Writing and Life.* New York: Anchor Books. Highly recommended: readable and engaging. This is packed with good advice.

Le Guin, U. (1998) *Steering the Craft: Exercises and Discussions On Story Writing for the Lone Navigator or the Mutinous Crew.* Portland, OR: Eighth Mountain. This book about writing fiction offers a combination of reflection, sample prose extracts and exercises. It ties in well with Francine Prose's *Reading Like a* Writer (see below) in that the exercises focus on form and structure. Some people find the exercises mechanistic, others have found the demand to write, say, without punctuation, or with a focus on the sound created by the prose liberating and intriguing. Make of it what you will!

Lowry, B. (2008) *Juicy Writing: Inspiration and Techniques for Young Writers*. Crows Nest, NSW: Allen & Unwin. This book is aimed at young writers and can be used as such. Some teachers have used the ideas quite extensively and successfully with their classes. It is crammed with good, simple ideas and is a good place to begin. Sometimes one just needs a way of getting a workshop plan started.

Morley, D. (2007) *The Cambridge Introduction to Creative Writing*. Cambridge: Cambridge University Press. This book invites the reader to reflect on process as well as on producing writing. There are chapters on fiction, non-fiction and poetry and a good number of ideas for getting started. See also: http://www.davidmorley.org.uk/

Prose, Francine (2007) *Reading Like a Writer*. New York: HarperCollins. This is a book about reading and writing in equal measure. Francine Prose analyses the work of novelists by looking closely at their use of language and in so doing draws attention to their skills as writers. Each chapter focuses on a different element of prose fiction, beginning with words, then sentences and on to details, gesture and reading for courage. It is an immensely readable and thought-provoking book.

Queneau, R. (translated by Wright, B.) (2009) *Exercises in Style*. Richmond, Surrey: One World Classics Ltd. This is a guide to literary forms demonstrated through the retelling of the same story ninety-nine times. It is provocative and funny. Adults and A level students have enjoyed the writing that it has prompted.

Sansom, P. (1994) *Writing Poems*. Newcastle upon Tyne: Bloodaxe Books. Peter Sansom is an excellent workshop leader and we encourage you to seek out his workshops (see below). You can learn a lot directly from him and through this book. The exercises at the end would keep you going for quite a while.

Schneider Pat (2003) *Writing Alone and With Others*. Oxford & New York: Oxford University Press. This is another book full of good observations and plenty of ideas for writing – alone and together, as the title suggests.

Stillman, P. (1989) *Families Writing*. Cincinnati, Ohio: Writer's Digest Books. We are pleased to see that this book is still in print, in a second edition. It is designed for use by families and is, therefore, great for parent–child workshops. It also has plenty of ideas that we have used very successfully with adult writers and that can be easily translated to the classroom.

Wilson, A., with Hughes, S. (eds.) (1998) *The Poetry Book for Primary Schools*. London: The Poetry Society. Yates, C. (1999) *Jumpstart: Poetry in the Secondary School*. London: The Poetry Society. These two good books from The Poetry Society are filled with practical ideas that work equally as well with adults as with young people.

Wood, M. (2001) *The Pocket Muse: Ideas and Inspiration for Writing*. Cincinnati: Writers Digest Books. This pocket-sized book is filled with photographs, horoscopes and prompts to write and organise your writing life. Try these: 'Use the following verbs in any way you wish: racket snug green spoon boggle snake.', 'You have to be willing to write badly.' and 'A character arrives at work to find her chair missing. What happened to it?'

Websites

Anthony Wilson's blog: www.anthonywilsonpoetry.com. Kick-start your day with this essential and popular online read.

The Arvon Foundation: www.arvonfoundation.org, runs writing courses throughout the year at four residential centres. There are special rates for teachers and opportunities for you to take groups of students for residential writing courses.

The Book Trust: Look at the section, 'Everybody Writes', which includes advice from writers, competitions, a writer in residence: booktrust.org.uk

Centre for Literacy in Primary Education: www.clpe.org.uk

The National Association for the Teaching of English: http://www.nate.org.uk/

National Association of Writers in Education (NAWE): www.nawe.co.uk

The National Writing Project (UK): www.nwp.org.uk

The National Writing Project (USA): www.nwp.org

Nottingham Writers' Studio: www.nottinghamwritersstudio.co.uk

The Poetry Archive: http://www.poetryarchive.org/poetryarchive/home.do

The Poetry Business: http://www.poetrybusiness.co.uk/. Founded and run by Ann and Peter Sansom, based in Sheffield, and generating publications, a poetry magazine, a whole range of courses. Poetry Business Writing Days are (usually) held on the last Saturday of each month in Sheffield.

The Poetry Society: http://www.poetrysociety.org.uk/. Poetry Class: http://www.poetryclass.poetrysociety.org.uk/. This is a part of the Poetry Society website and contains a wealth of information for writing teachers, including lesson plans, interviews, resources and useful links.

The Poetry Trust: www.thepoetrytrust.org. News here of the most inspirational poetry festival in the country and a generous offering of podcasts and resources.

The Scottish Poetry Library: www.scottishpoetrylibrary.org.uk

Teachers and Writers Collaborative: www.twc.org. This New York-based organisation is full of ideas and resources. The organisation was set up to get writers into New York schools.

University of Texas at Austin: http://www.learningrecord.org/. Here you will find the framework for the Learning Record mentioned in Chapter 16.

The Writers' Centre, Norwich: www.writerscentrenorwich.org.uk

The Write Team, part of the Bath Literary Festival, has excellent resources: www.bathfestivals.org.uk/

Index